CHRISTMAS
Activity Book

CHRISTMAS
Activity Book

90+ Games-mazes, coloring, word search
puzzles and more for kids ages 4-8

Mare Robbins

YOUNG
SCHOLAR BOOKS

Interior and Cover Design: Mare Robbins

ISBN: 978-1-63589-821-7

NOTE TO PARENTS

Hello, I'm Mare Robbins. Little ones are curious by nature and will gravitate to whatever keeps their attention. Devices with all their lights, bells, and whistles are desirable. But, books that encourage participation, like this one, will help strike a moderate balance between book time and screen time, the old and the new.

A child is like a clean slate. As they grow and develop, they acquire new skills by observing, participating, and analyzing. This all comes together to lay a solid foundation for their success in life. It is essential that they have an accessible and available way to help them develop their minds and senses, even during Thanksgiving.

Christmas is a once-a-year celebration that brings families and friends together to socialize, and give thanks. Writing and reading are fundamental skills that children should learn as early as possible, and learning should not take a break during holidays. Christmas, presents an excellent opportunity to ensure that skills already learned are perfected as new ones are picked up.

Introducing, Christmas Activity Book for kids! It's full of Christmas themed games to entertain your child. Images to color, mazes to go through, tracing and handwriting sessions, patterns to identify, word search, dot to dot, scissor skills section, and lots more!

All your little one needs are crayons, a pair of scissors and a can-do attitude. This activity book will keep your child focused and engaged, with little guidance from a parent or caregiver. Working with crayons, and a pair of scissors, helps improve your child's hand-eye coordination and dexterity.

Satisfaction in completing a task helps build confidence. There are 90 plus opportunities to do just that this Christmas!
Enjoy!

CONTENTS

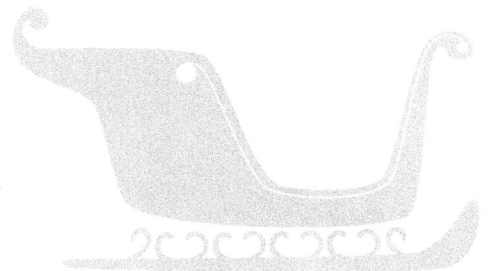

XMAS SELFIE WITH SANTA!

My vacation in pictures

Glue pics here.

SANTA'S HERE, YEA!

Guide Santa to the kids.

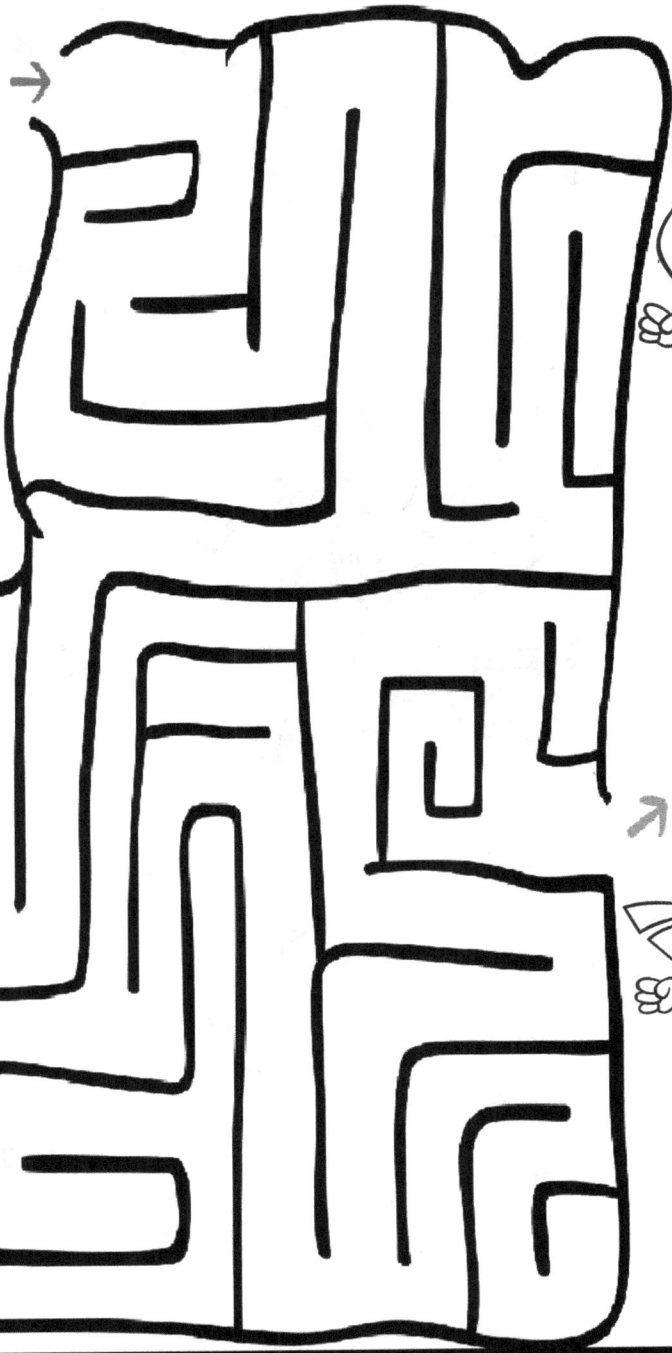

FROSTY THE SNOWMAN

Image and shadow match!

PRACTICE TRACING.

Trace and connect similar Christmas elements.

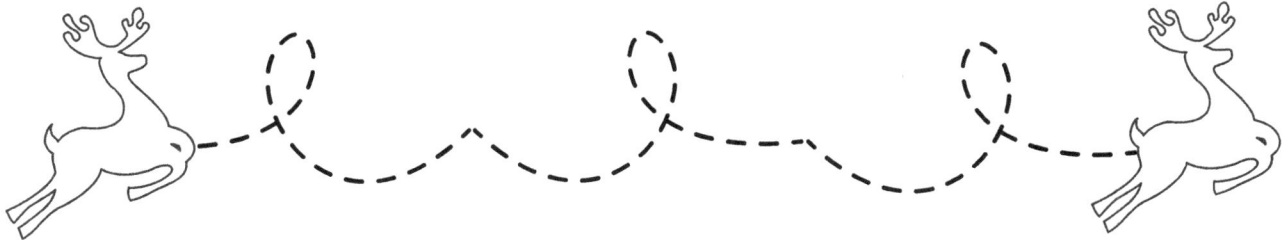

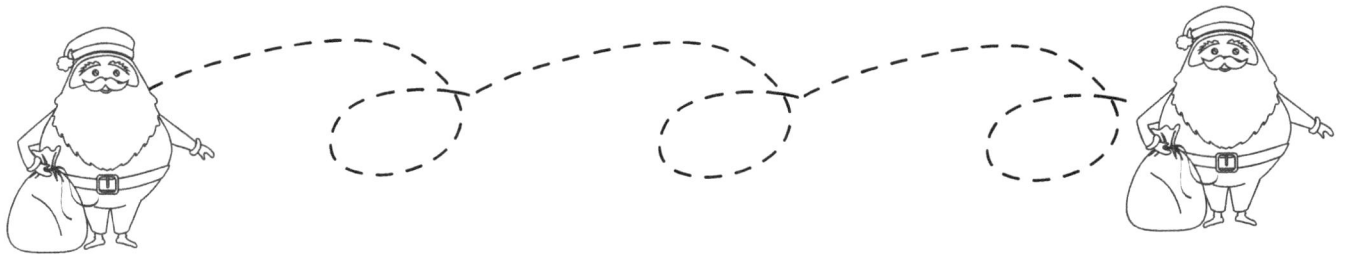

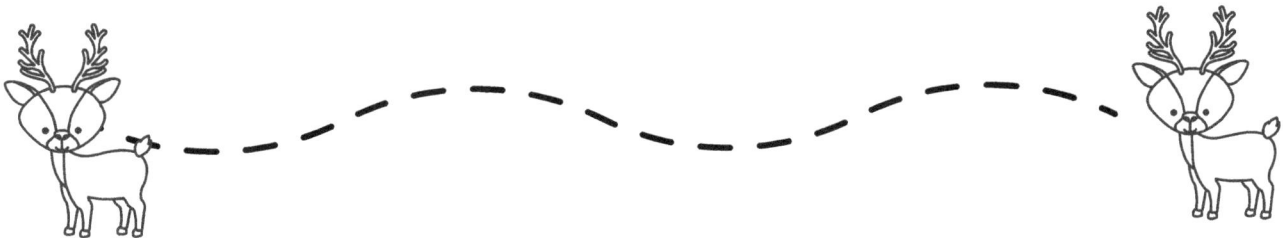

MATCHING IMAGES

Draw a line to match images that look the same.

GUIDE SANTA!

Help Santa get to the house

SYMMETRY DRAWING

Use the grid to draw the other side of the Christmas bulb

WHO GETS THE GIFTS?

A, B or C?. Trace the line puzzles

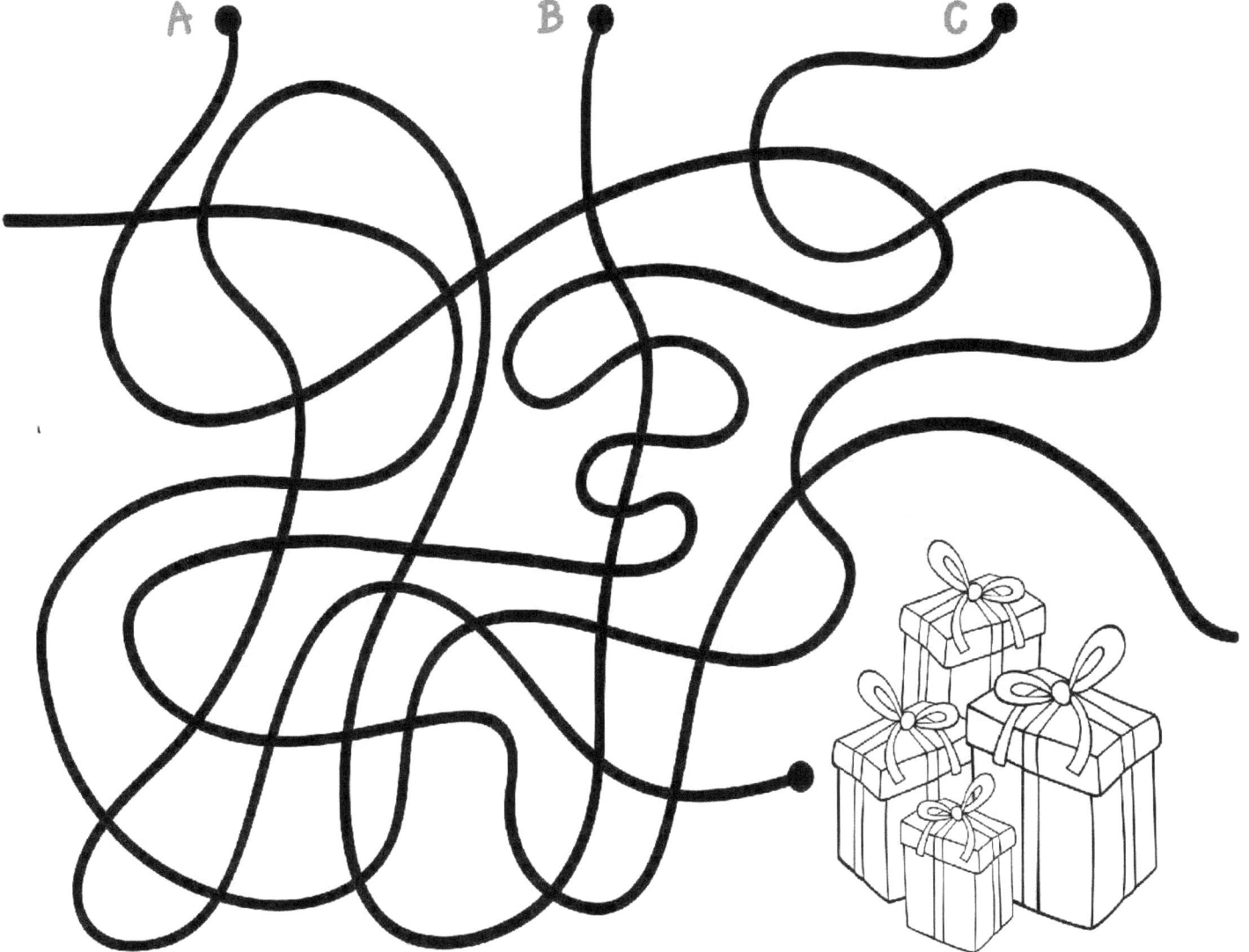

PRESENT DELIVERY!

Guide Santa to the house.

SANTA'S SHADOW.

Find the right Santa

SYMMETRY DRAWING

Use the grid to draw the other side of the Christmas present.

TREE ORNAMENTS.

Help the little girl get to the Christmas Tree

CHRISTMAS COLORS.

Identify and color the Christmas elements.

RED

ORANGE

YELLOW
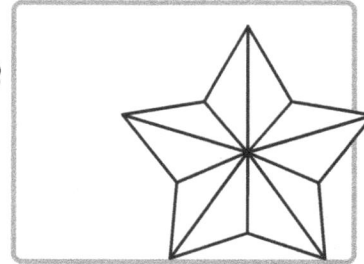

GREEN

BLUE

PURPLE

PINK

TORQUOISE

GRAY

BROWN

WHITE

BLACK

SANTA CLAUS.

color me.

HO HO HO!

HO

ELF.

Your presents are coming! Color me.

CHRISTMAS STOCKING.

Color Me!

Aa angel	**Bb** bell	**Cc** candy cane	**Dd** dancer
Ee elf	**Ff** fruitcake	**Gg** garland	**Hh** holly
Ii ice skate	**Jj** jingle bells	**Kk** kings	**Ll** lights
Mm mittens	**Nn** North Pole	**Oo** ornaments	**Pp** presents
Qq quinoa	**Rr** ribbon	**Ss** Santa	**Tt** tree
Uu upside down cake	**Vv** vegetables	**Ww** wrapping paper	**Xx** xmas
Yy yule log	**Zz** zucchini	**CHRISTMAS ALPHABET CHART**	

A IS FOR ANGEL

. Color the image.

Aa

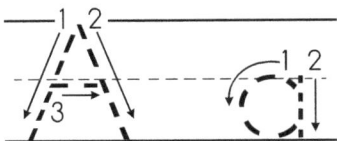

Trace and write the uppercase letter

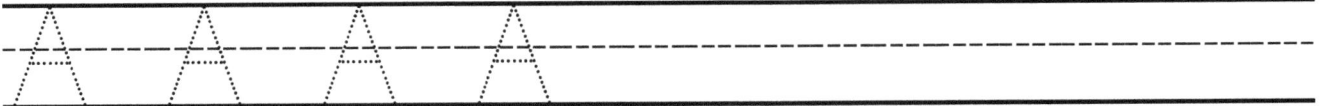

A A A A

Trace and write the lowercase letter

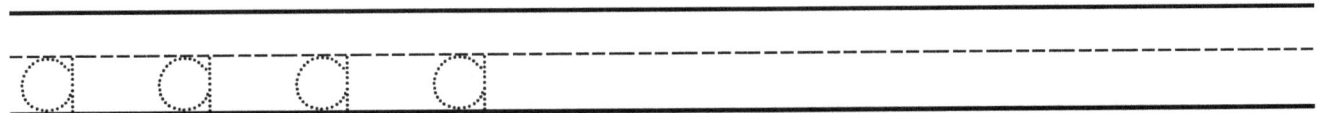

a a a a

B IS FOR BELL

Circle the correct bell shadow

Bb

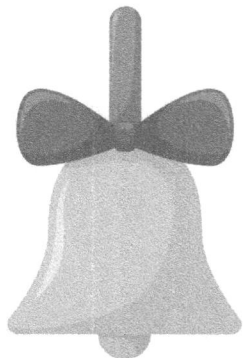

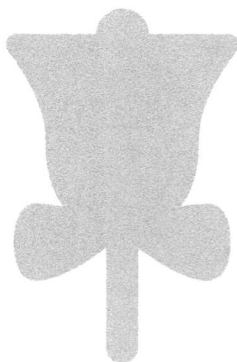

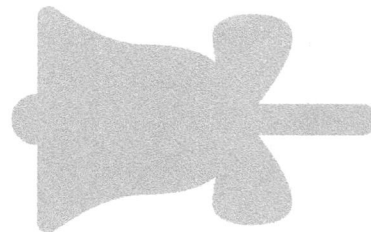

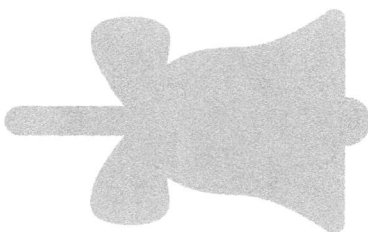

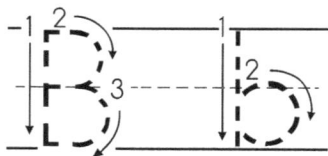

Trace and write the uppercase letter

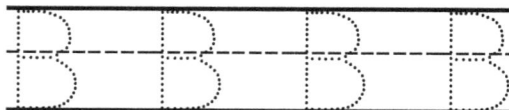

B B B B

Trace and write the lowercase letter

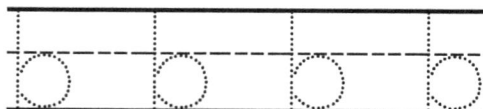

b b b b

C IS FOR CANDY CANE

How many Candy canes do you see?

C c

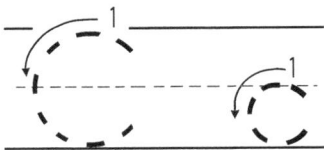

Trace and write the uppercase letter

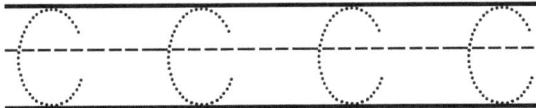

C C C C

Trace and write the lowercase letter

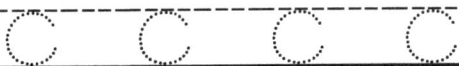

c c c c

D IS FOR DANCER

Color by Alphabet

A - Red
B - Brown
C - Green
D - Yellow

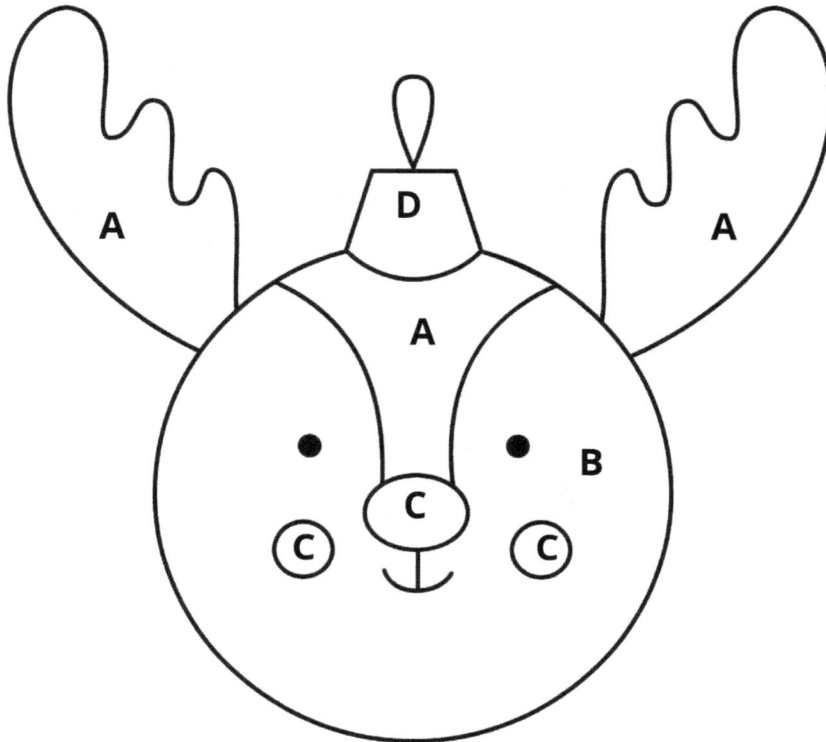

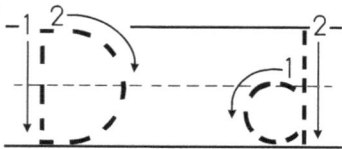

Dd

Trace and write the uppercase letter

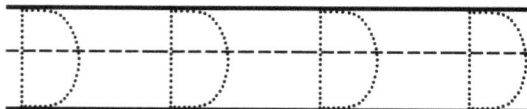

Trace and write the lowercase letter

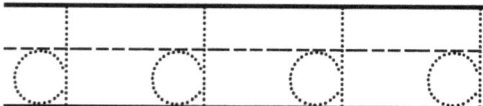

E IS FOR ELF

Help the elf load Santa's sleigh.

Ee

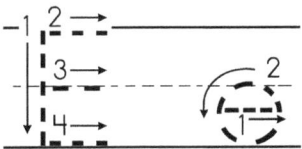

Trace and write the uppercase letter

Trace and write the lowercase letter

F IS FOR FRUITCAKE

Name the fruits on the cake. Color the image

Ff

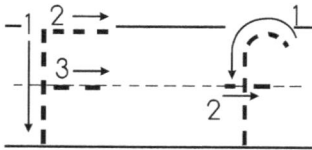

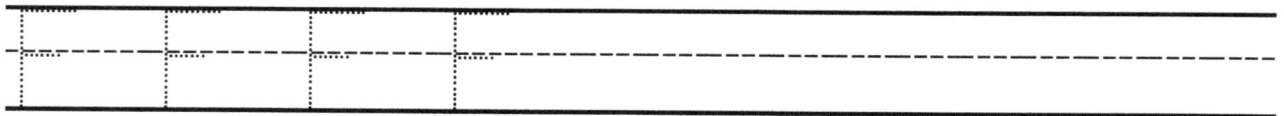

Trace and write the lowercase letter

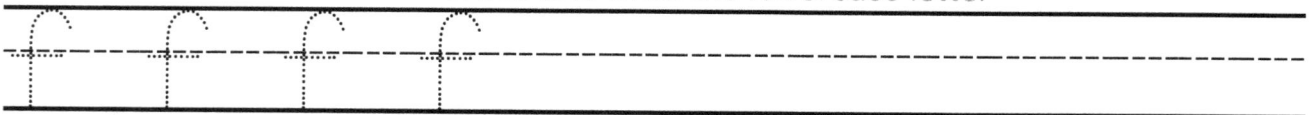

G Is for Garland

Trace and color.

Gg

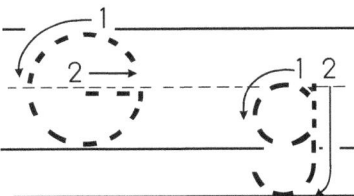

Trace and write the uppercase letter

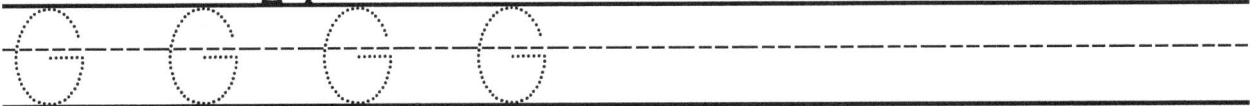

G G G G

Trace and write the lowercase letter

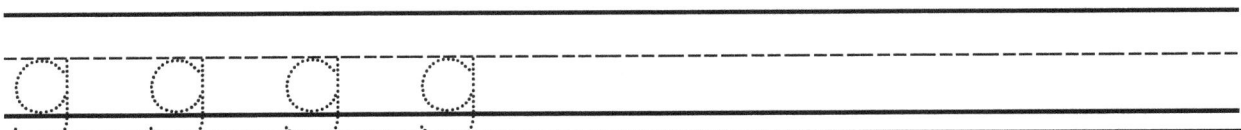

g g g g

23

H IS FOR HOLLY

Help the Elf get the holly

Hh

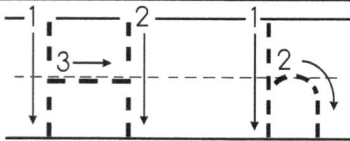

Trace and write the uppercase letter

Trace and write the lowercase letter

I IS FOR ICE SKATE

Trace a path through the maze. Use the skates

Ii

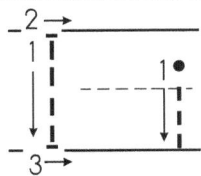

Trace and write the uppercase letter

Trace and write the lowercase letter

J IS FOR JINGLE BELLS
Color the bells

Jj

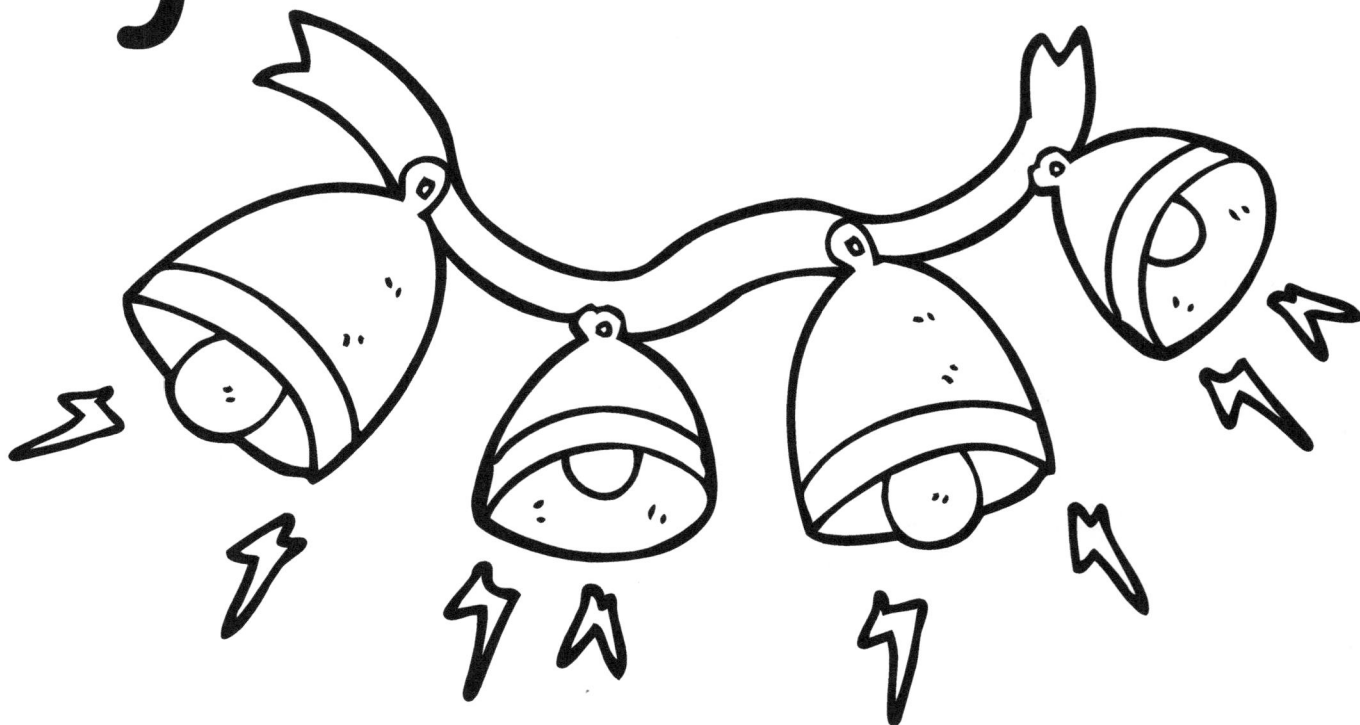

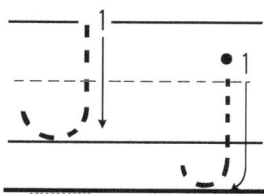

Trace and write the uppercase letter

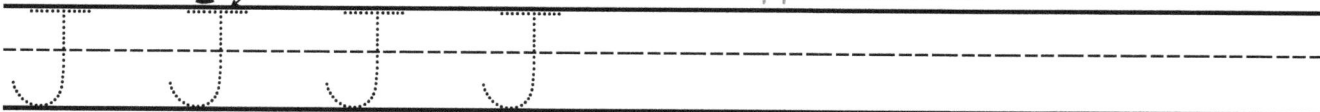

Trace and write the lowercase letter

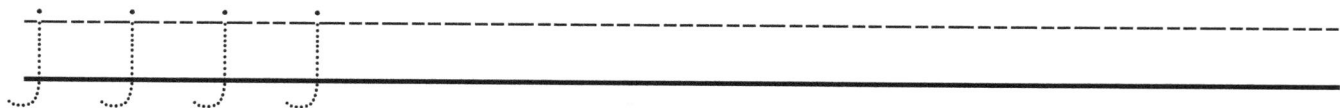

K IS FOR KINGS

Guide the 3 kings to the manger

Kk

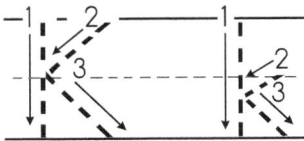

Trace and write the uppercase letter

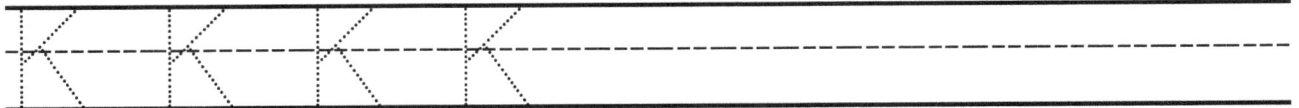

Trace and write the lowercase letter

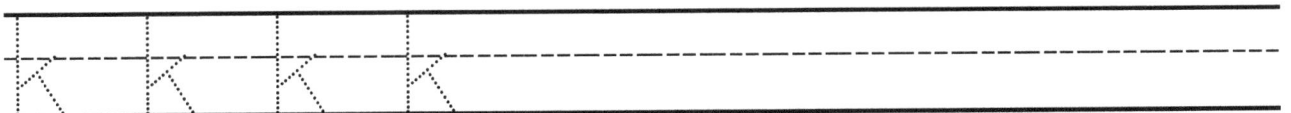

L Is for Lights

Connect the dots A-L-l. Color the bulbs

L l

K
L
J
I
L
I
I
L
L
D
E
C
F
A
B
G
H

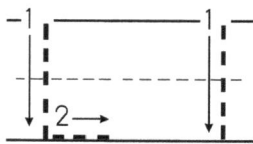

Trace and write the uppercase letter

Trace and write the lowercase letter

M is for Mittens

Match the pairs of mittens. Spot the odd one out.

Mm

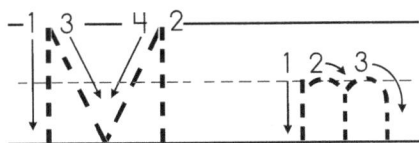

Trace and write the uppercase letter

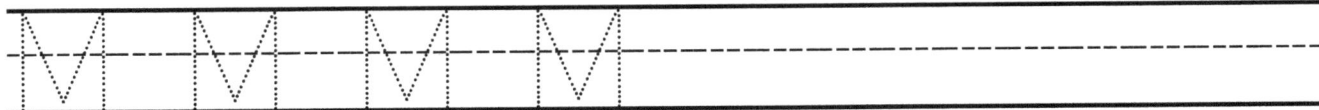

Trace and write the lowercase letter

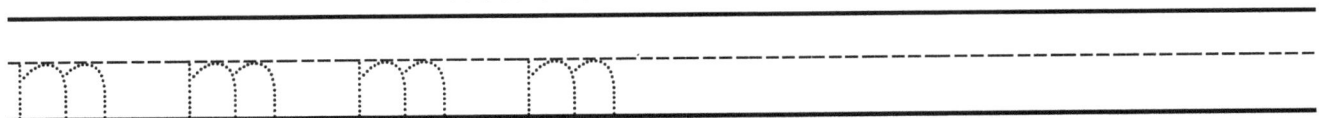

N Is for North Pole

Trace everyonel to where they live. Where is Santa's home?

Nn

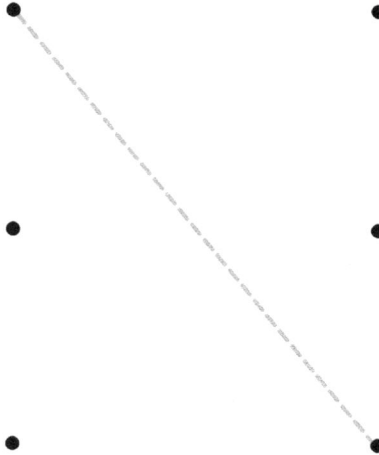

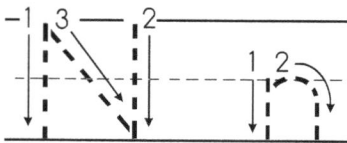

Trace and write the uppercase letter

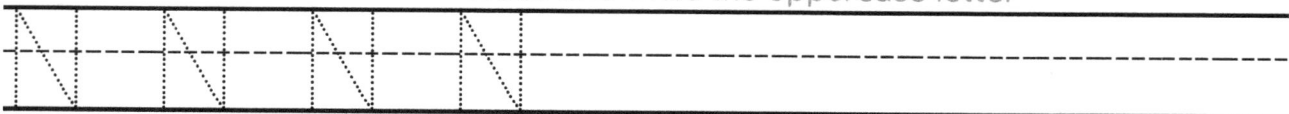

N N N N

Trace and write the lowercase letter

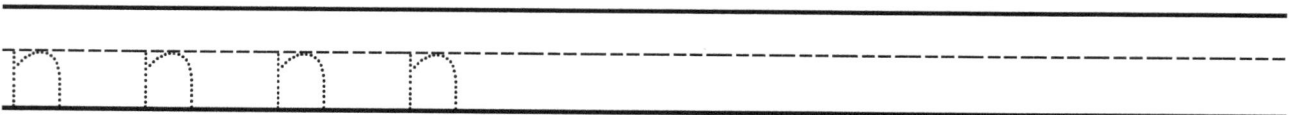

n n n n

O Is for Ornament

Find two identical ornaments

O o

1 2 3 4

5 6 7 8

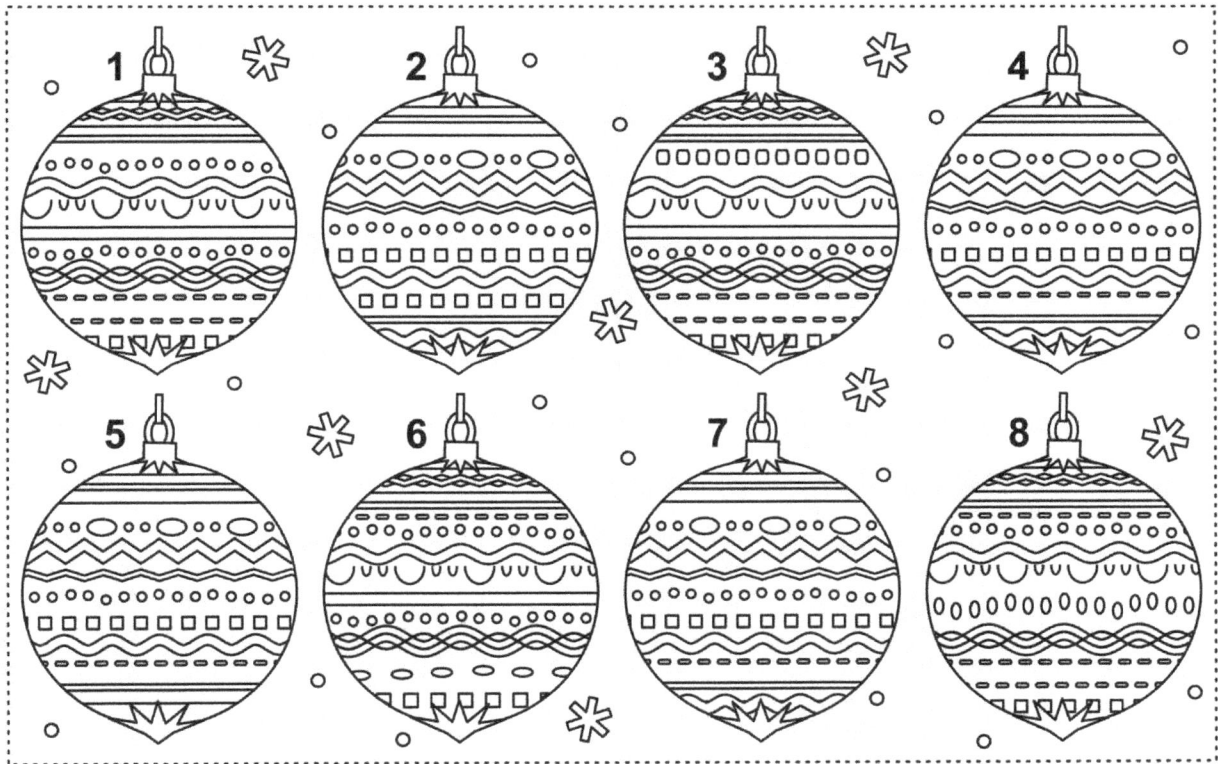

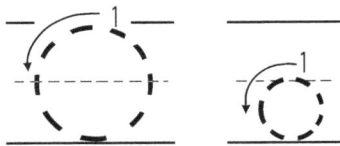

Trace and write the uppercase letter

Trace and write the lowercase letter

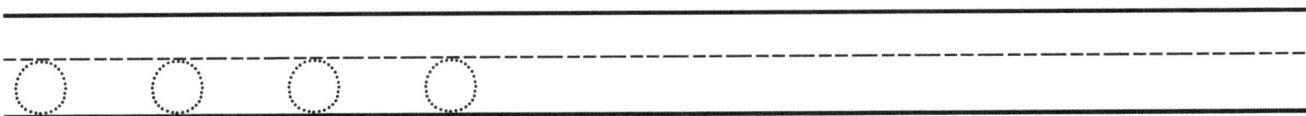

P IS FOR PRESENT

Trace and color.

P p

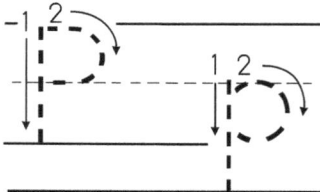

Trace and write the uppercase letter

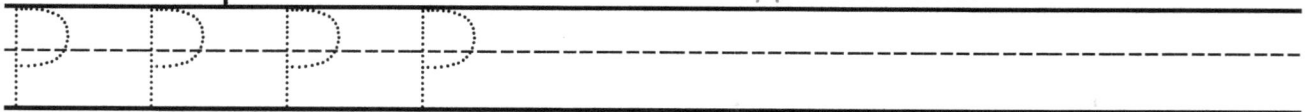

P P P P

Trace and write the lowercase letter

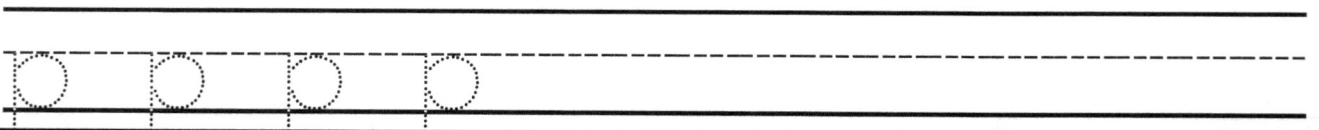

p p p p

Q IS FOR QUINOA

Help Santa get to the Quinoa Salad!

Qq

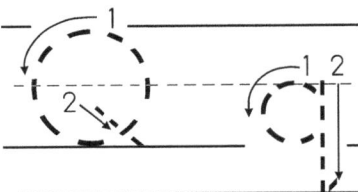

Trace and write the uppercase letter

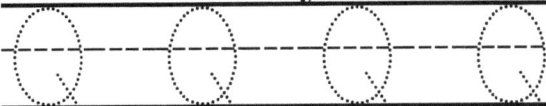

Trace and write the lowercase letter

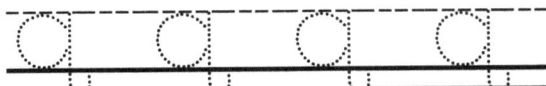

R IS FOR RIBBON

Circle the correct ribbon shadow

Rr

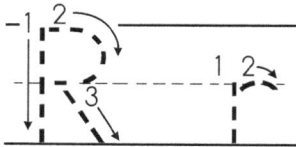

Trace and write the uppercase letter

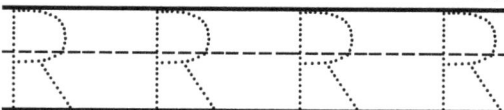

R R R R

Trace and write the lowercase letter

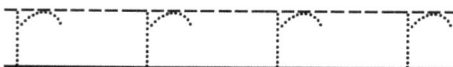

r r r r

S IS FOR SANTA

Match each Santa to his shadow

Ss

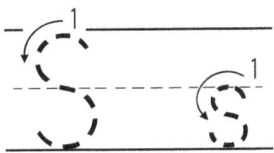

Trace and write the uppercase letter

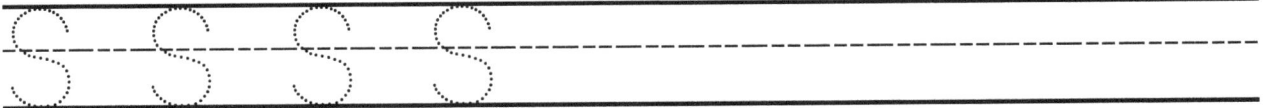

S S S S

Trace and write the lowercase letter

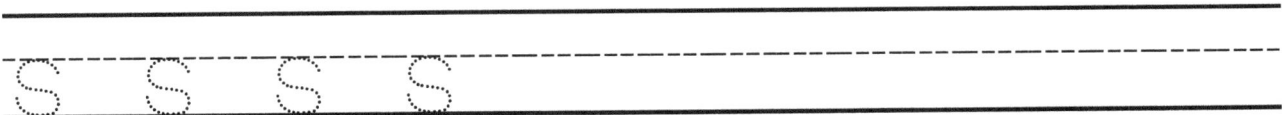

s s s s

T Is for Tree

Follow the stars to the top of the Christmas tree. Color the stars yellow

Tt

Trace and write the uppercase letter

Trace and write the lowercase letter

U IS FOR UPSIDE-DOWN CAKE

Color the uppercase U yellow, lowercase u red. Pick any color for T.

Uu

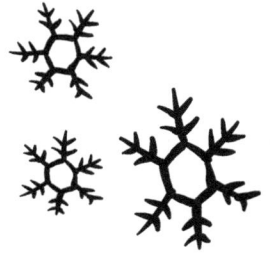

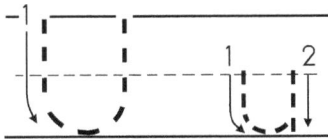

Trace and write the uppercase letter

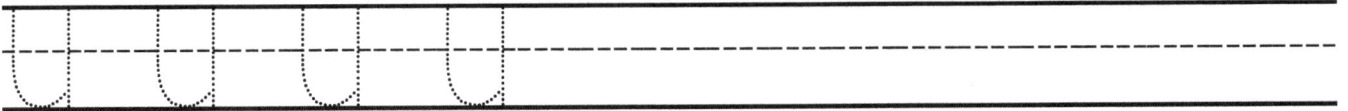

Trace and write the lowercase letter

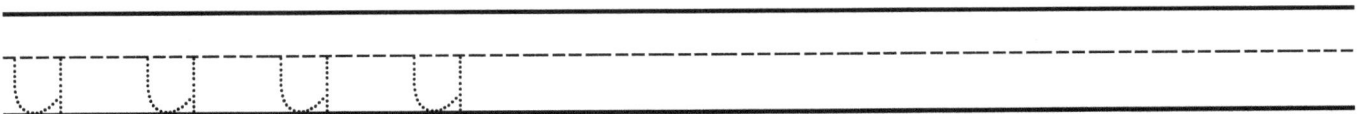

V IS FOR VEGETABLE

Circle the vegetable that comes next.

Vv

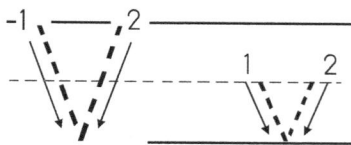

Trace and write the uppercase letter

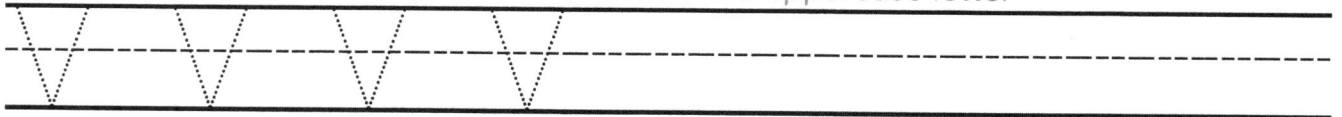

Trace and write the lowercase letter

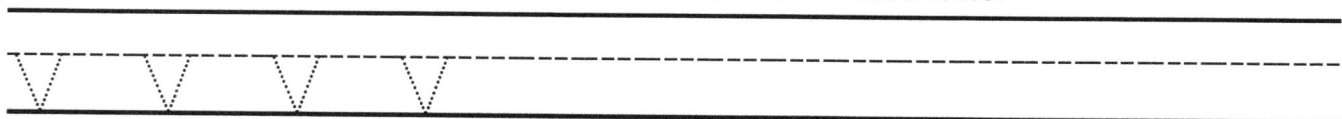

W IS FOR WRAPPING PAPER

Color the wrapped gifts

Ww

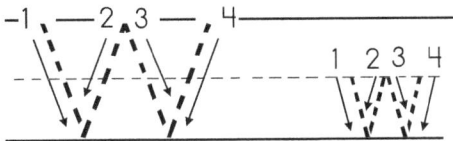

Trace and write the uppercase letter

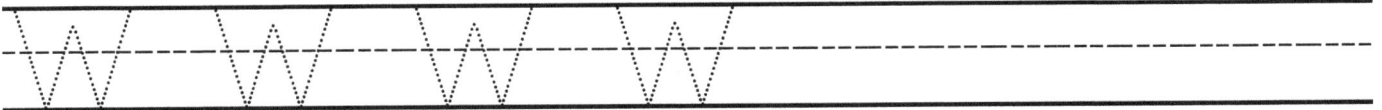

Trace and write the lowercase letter

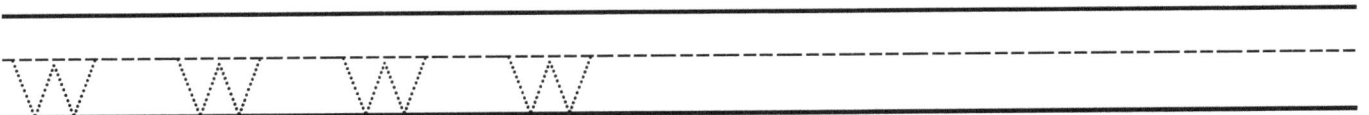

X Is for Xmas
Guide Santa to the Xmas party

Xx

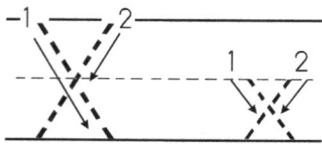

Trace and write the uppercase letter

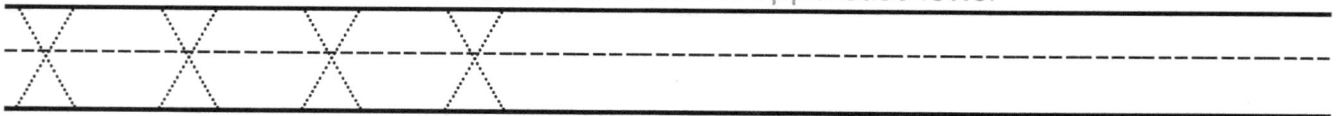

Trace and write the lowercase letter

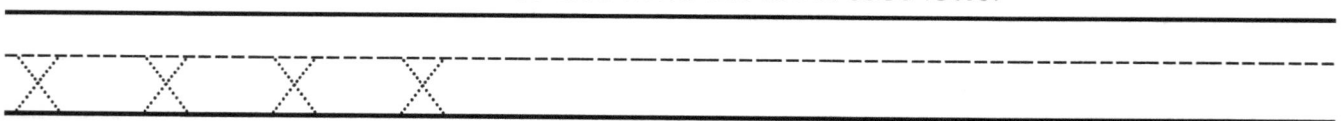

Y IS FOR YULE LOG

Connect the dots A-Y-y for your Christmas dessert

Yy

V
W
X
U
Y
y
y
T
Y
Y
y
S
J
K
E
D
A
I
Y
F
B
C
R
G
H
L
y
Q
M
Y
N
O
P

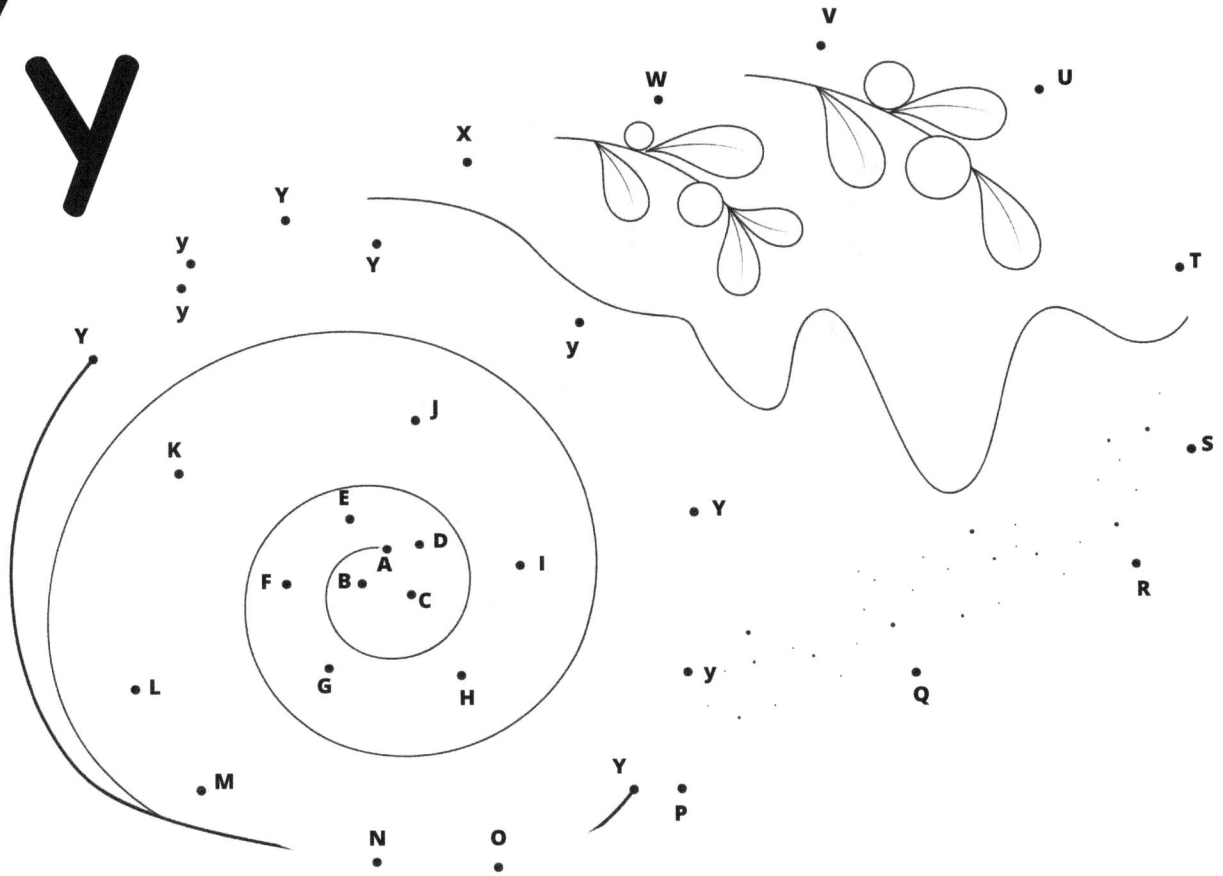

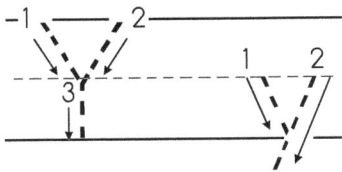

Trace and write the uppercase letter

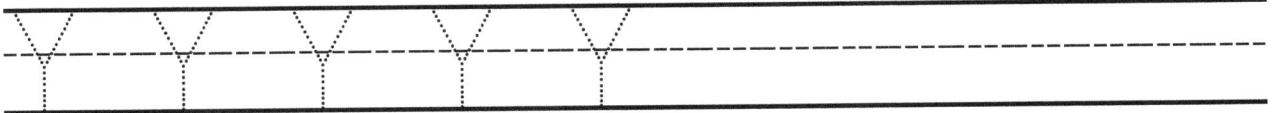

Y Y Y Y Y

Trace and write the lowercase letter

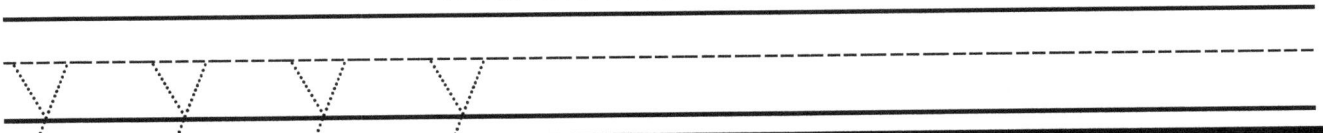

y y y y

Z IS FOR ZUCCHINI

Help the Snow man get to his favorite vegetable

Zz

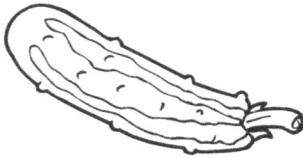

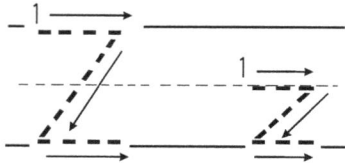

Trace and write the uppercase letter

Trace and write the lowercase letter

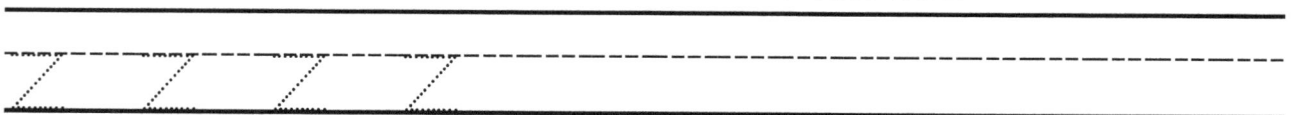

CHRISTMAS SIGHT WORDS

Practice writing words below

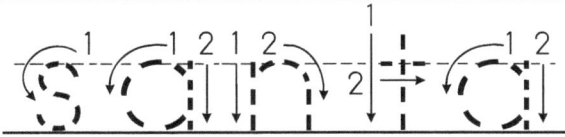

santa

santa santa

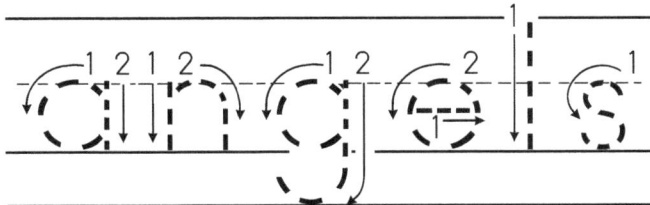

Trace and write the word below

angels

angels angels

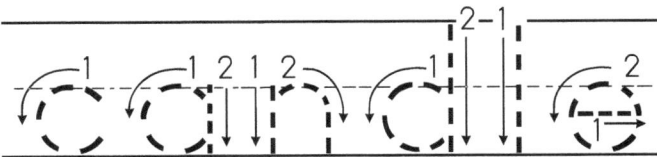

Trace and write the word below

candle

candle candle

Trace and write the word below

CHRISTMAS SIGHT WORDS

Practice writing words below

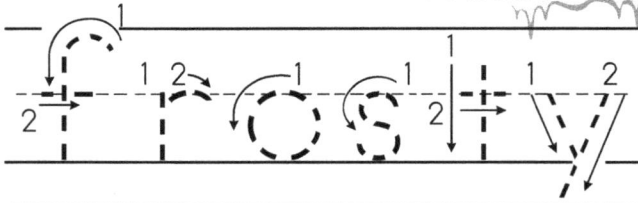

frosty

Trace and write the word below

frosty   frosty

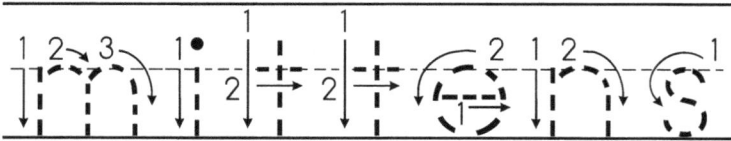

mittens

Trace and write the word below

mittens mittens

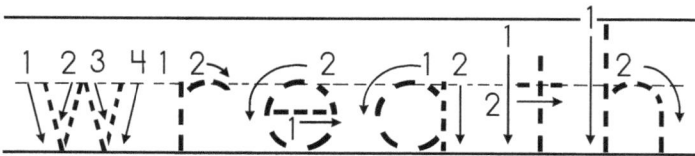

wreath

Trace and write the word below

wreath wreath

CHRISTMAS SIGHT WORDS
Practice writing words below

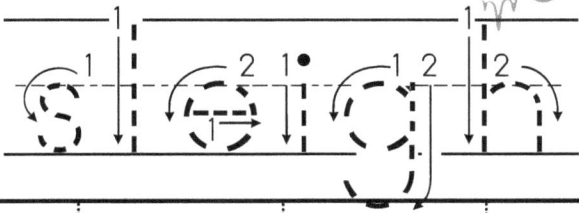

sleigh

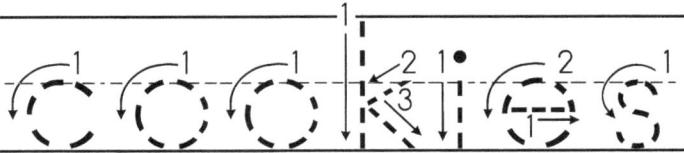

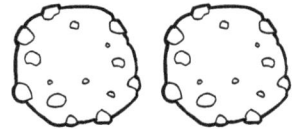

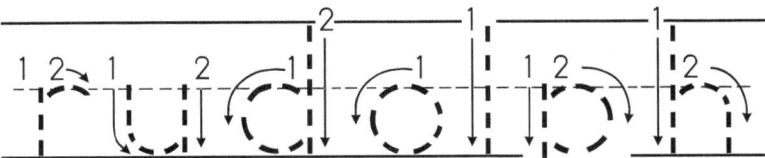

Trace and write the word below

sleigh sleigh

cookies

Trace and write the word below

cookies cookies

rudolph

Trace and write the word below

rudolph rudolph

WHAT'S IN THE PICTURE FRAME?

Nothing? Zero? You are correct!

0

Trace and write the number below

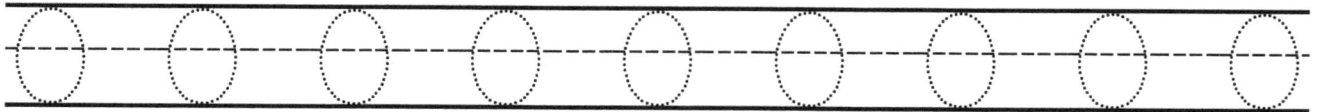

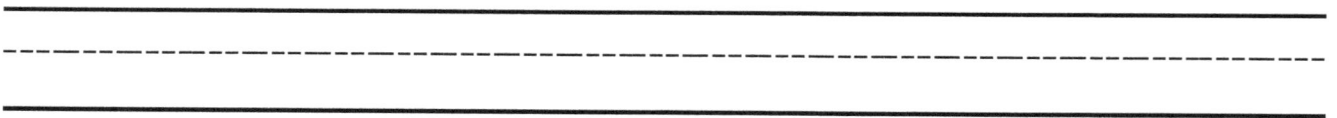

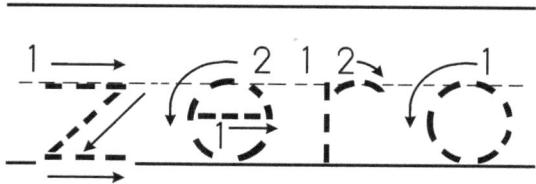

Trace and write the word below

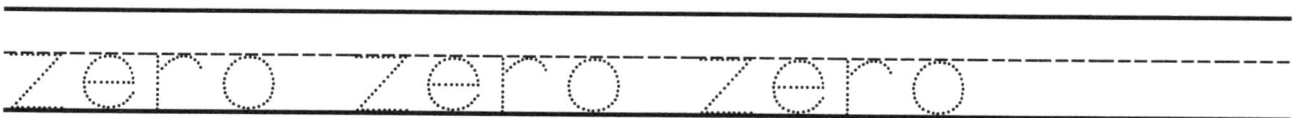

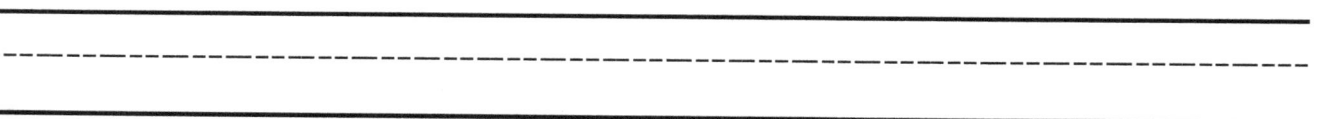

zero

WHICH GIFT?
Color the gift with 1 written on it

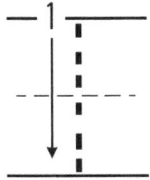

I

5 2 3

4 6 1

1

Trace and write the number below

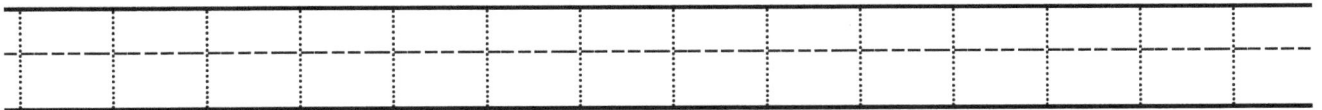

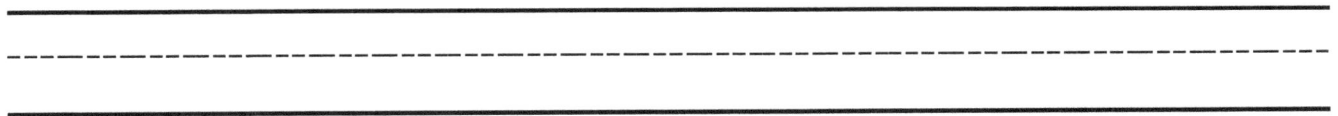

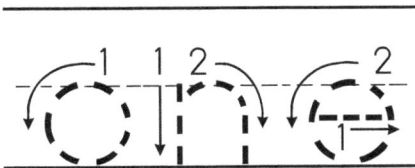

one

one

Trace and write the word below

one one one one

HOW MANY ELVES?

Shade the circle with the right number of elves

2

1 2 3

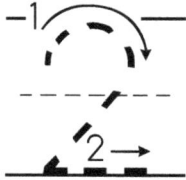

Trace and write the number below

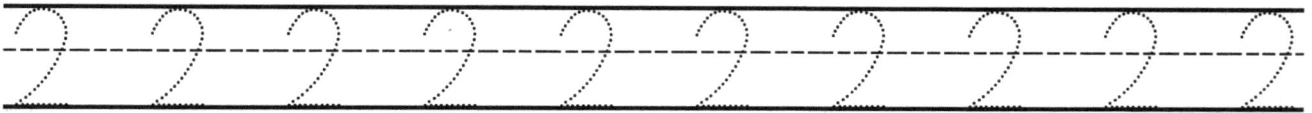

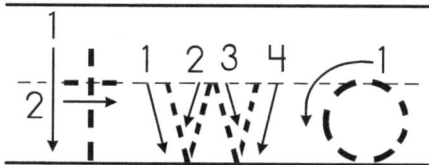

2 2 2 2 2 2 2 2 2 2

Trace and write the word below

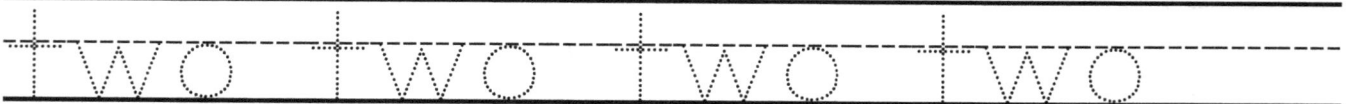

two

two two two two

Find and circle 3 stockings

3

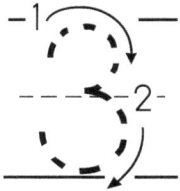

Trace and write the number below

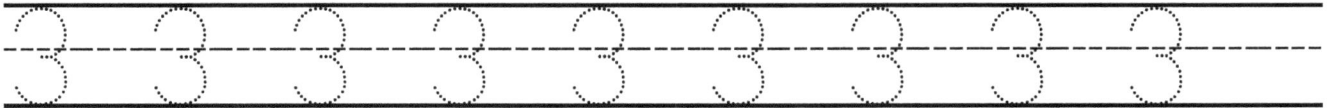

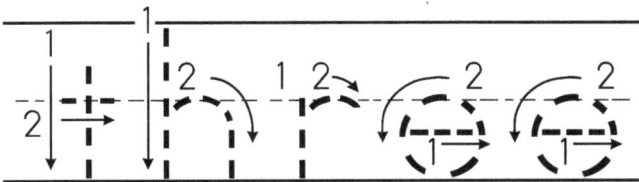

3 3 3 3 3 3 3 3 3

Trace and write the word below

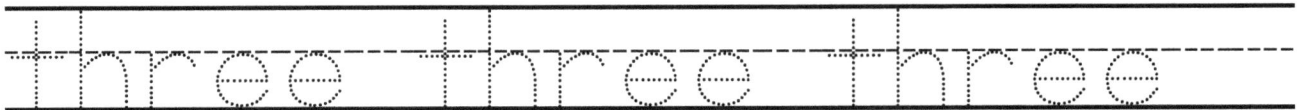

three

three three three

CHRISTMAS DINNER ROLL

1-4's dot to dot, to reveal a sweet dinner roll.

4

4
4   4
4   4   4
4   4   4   1
4   4   • 2
4   •
                • 3

•   • 4
4

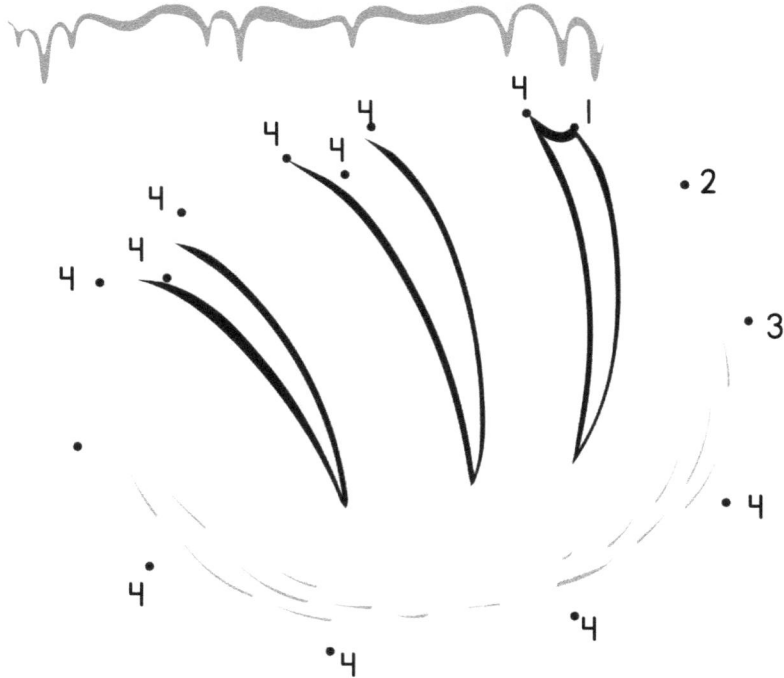

4   • 4
    • 4
Trace and write the number below

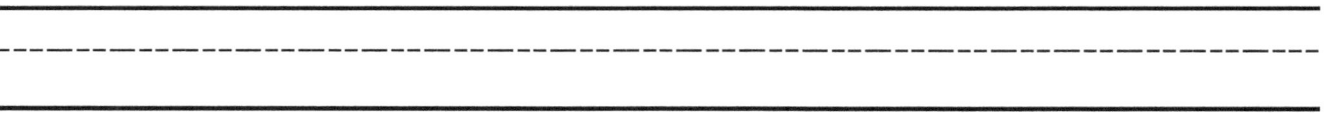

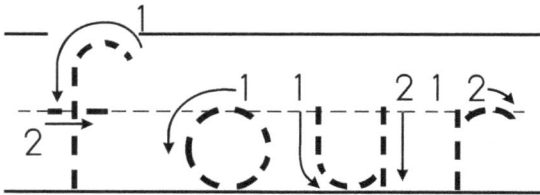

Trace and write the word below

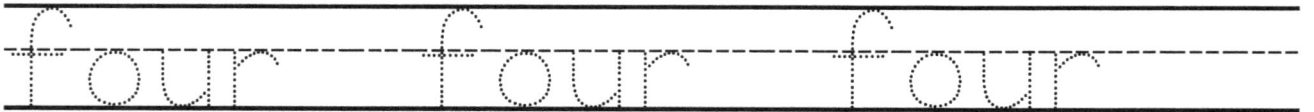

four   four   four

Snow Fight!

There are 5 differences. Circle each one.

5

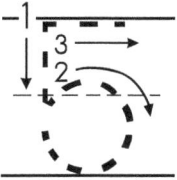

Trace and write the number below

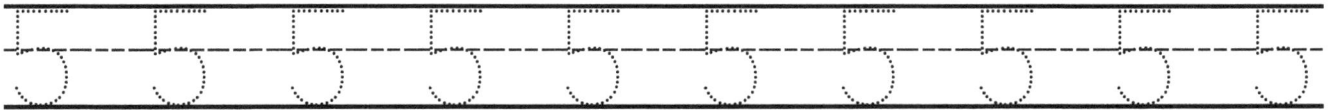

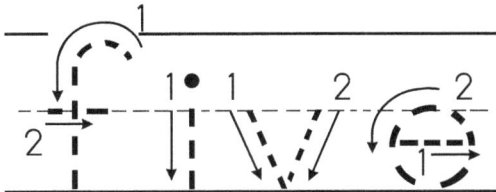

5 5 5 5 5 5 5 5 5 5

Trace and write the word below

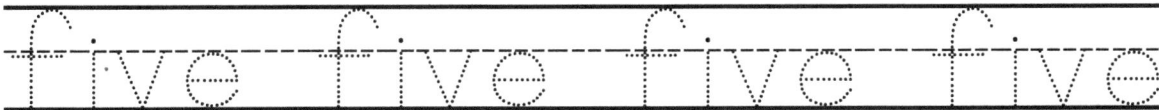

five five five five

LOST NOSE

6

Trace and write the number below

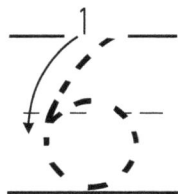

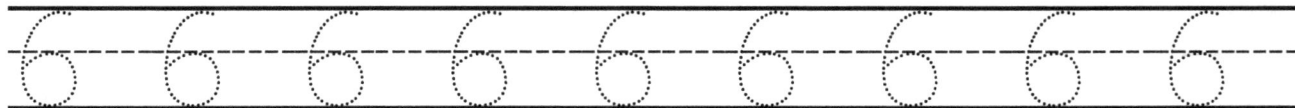

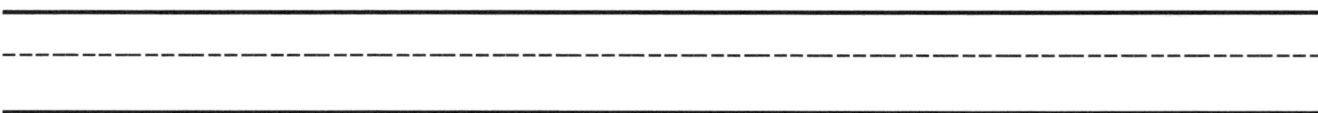

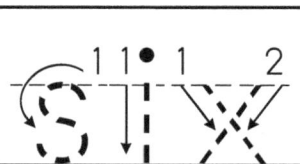

6 6 6 6 6 6 6 6 6

six

six

Trace and write the word below

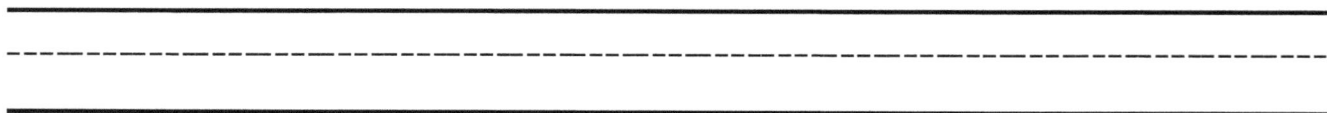

six six six six six

SANTA CONVENTION!

Find and circle 7 differences!

7

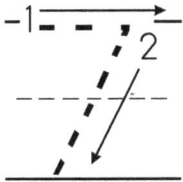

Trace and write the number below

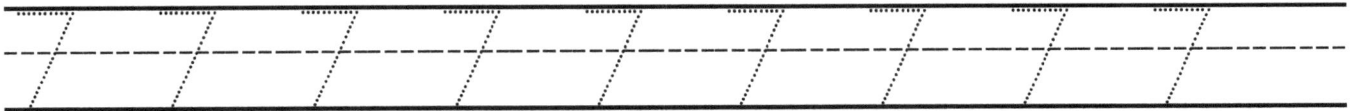

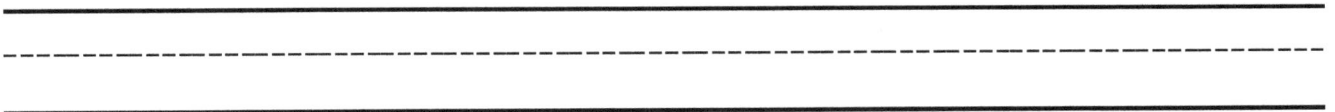

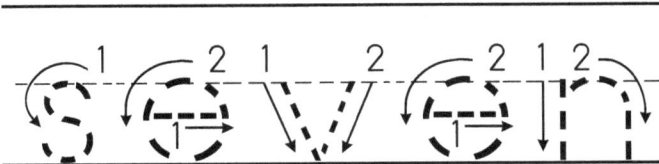

7 7 7 7 7 7 7 7

seven **seven**

Trace and write the word below

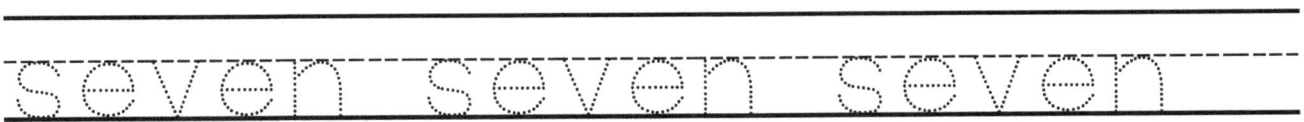

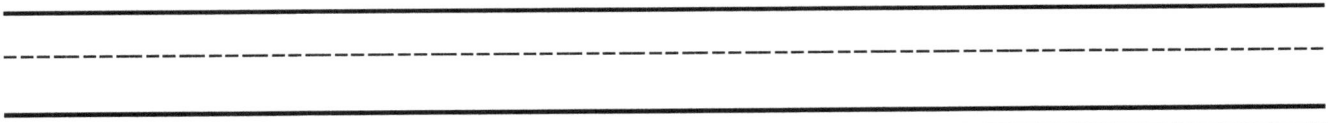

seven seven seven

COLOR BY NUMBER

Connect the dots 1-8-8

8

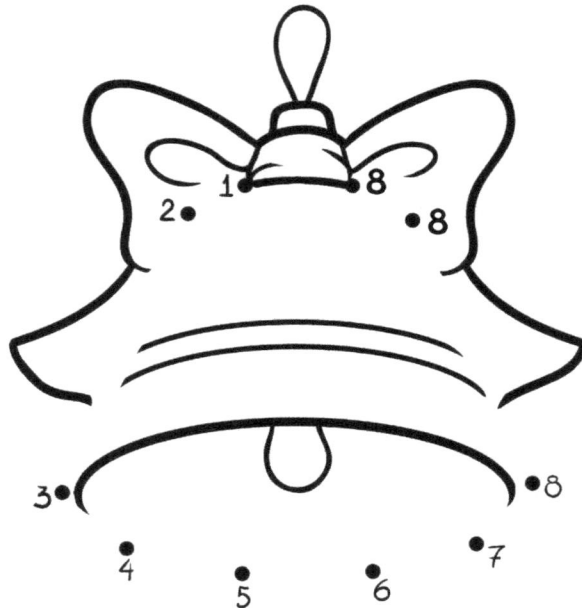

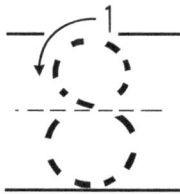

Trace and write the number below

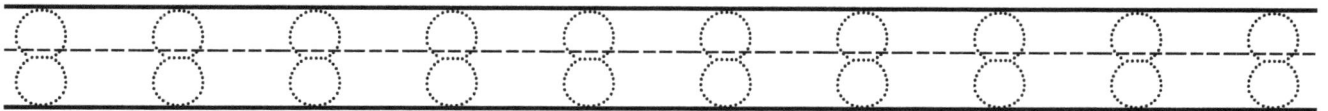

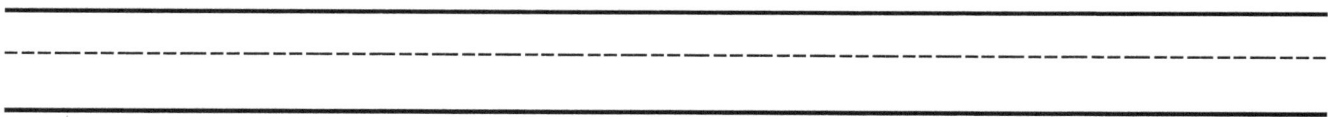

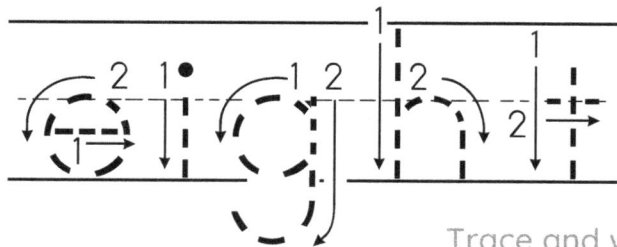

8 8 8 8 8 8 8 8 8 8

Trace and write the word below

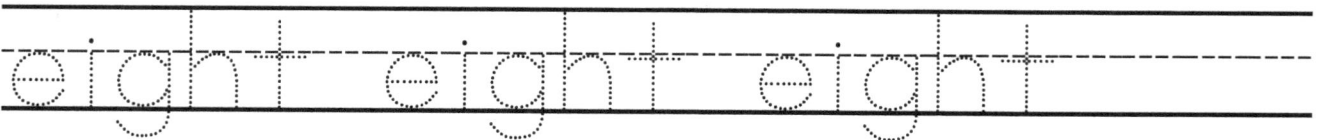

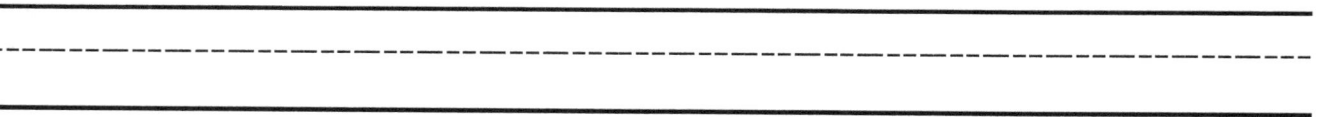

eight

eight eight eight

COUNTING TIME

How many Santa's are facing left, and right respectively?

q

Which one has 9?

LEFT | RIGHT

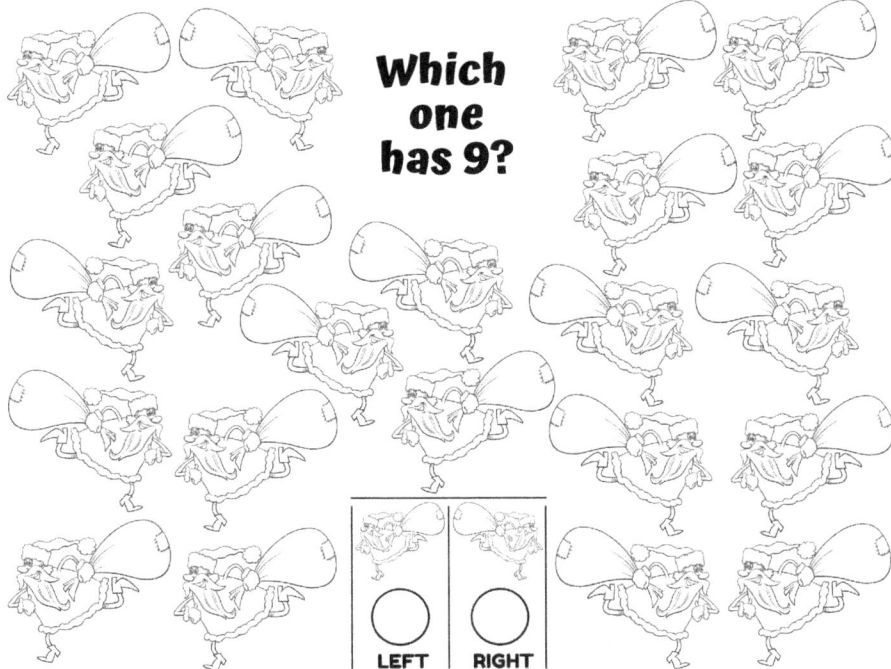

Trace and write the number below

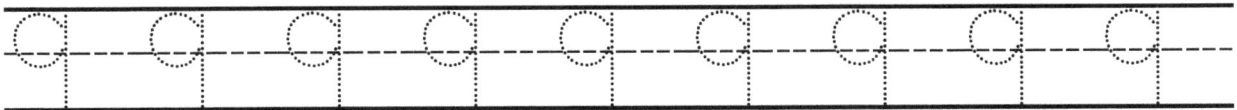

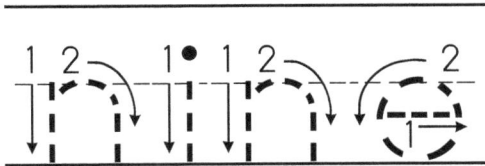

q q q q q q q q q q

Trace and write the word below

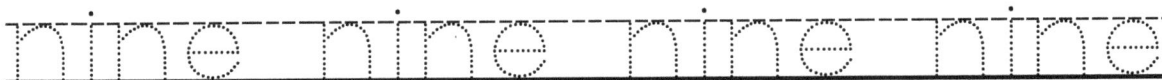

nine

nine

nine nine nine nine

TEN?

YES! Find 10 differences between the two pictures.

10

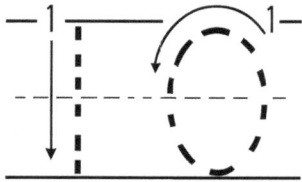

Trace and write the number below

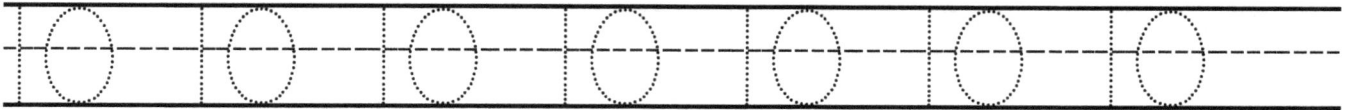

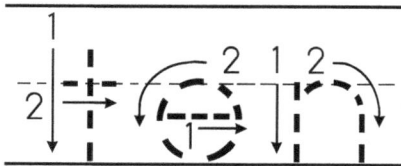

10 10 10 10 10 10 10

Trace and write the word below

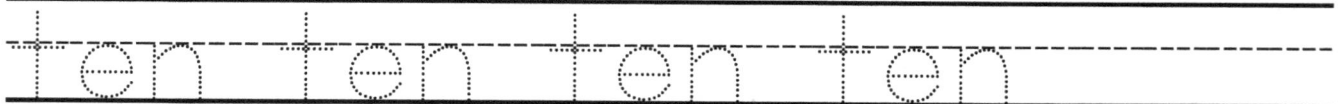

ten ten ten ten

CHRISTMAS BOWS.

Count and record

CHRISTMAS ELEMENTS

Count each row of images. Write the correct number in the circle.

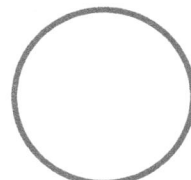

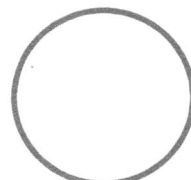

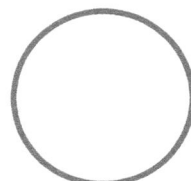

CANDLES, MITTENS, AND MORE!

Count the Christmas object in each box and mark the correct number

4   1   3   2   2   3   5   7

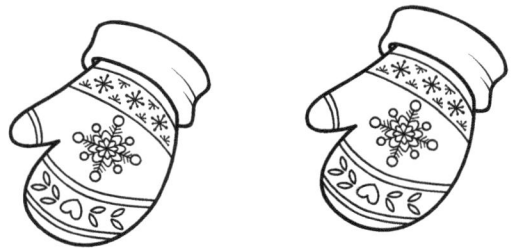

2   1   5   4   8   7   4   3

DOT-TO-DOT SANTA CLAUS

Connect the dots and color

TWO SETS OF SANTA?

Count the 2 Santa images. Record your number.

CHRISTMAS MUG.

connetc the dots 1 to 24, and color

23

24

1

2

3

22

4

21

5

20

6

7

19

8

18

9

17

10

11

16

12

15

14

13

CHRISTMAS PRESENT.

Compare the two images

Find 10 differences.

CHRISTMAS SINGING

Complete dot to dot, and color

FROSTY NEEDS HELP.

Help Frosty find his way out.

CHRISTMAS MITTENS.

Compare the two images

Find 10 differences.

BEGINNING LETTER

Identify each image out loud. Say the letter it begins with.
Color the letter it begins with.

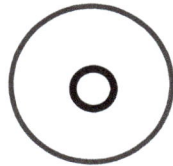

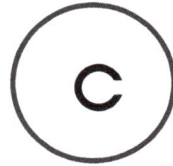

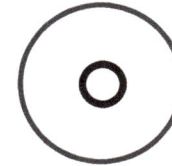

b	o	c	s
p	b	n	t
r	e	s	a
h	s	p	o
w	b	m	p

MATCH & TRACE

Name the image. Match the image with the first letter of the word.
Trace the uppercase and lowercase letters.

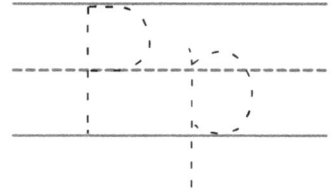

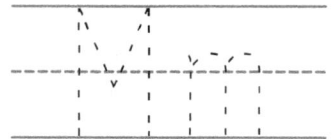

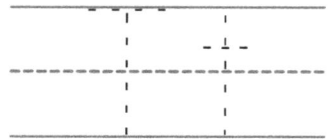

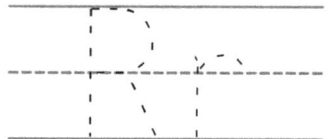

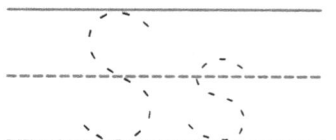

Pp

Mm

Ii

Rr

Ss

PRACTICE TRACING

Trace and connect words to Christmas elements.

cookie

mistletoe

reindeer

santa

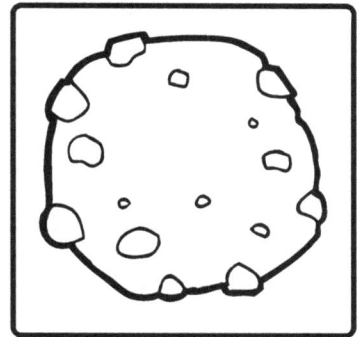

star

candy cane

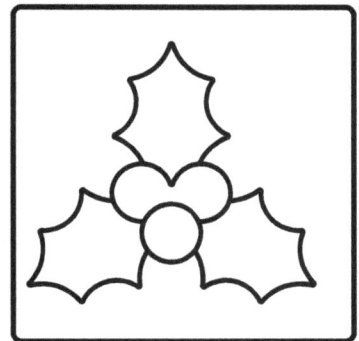

RHYMING WORDS

Circle the word that rhymes with the word inside the box.

sled		hug	bread
tree		flea	yam
sock	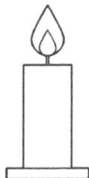	see	clock
candle		handle	bend
bell		shell	skid
wreath		pen	teeth

CHRISTMAS WORD SALAD

Identify the image. Unscramble the letters.

r i f

XMAS WORD SALAD

Identify the scene. Unscramble the words.

t	v	y	i	a	i	n	t

MISSING LETTERS

Identify each image below. Write the missing letter.

_weater

gif_

fro_ty

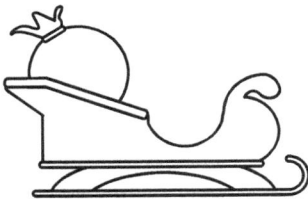
_leigh

sno_

sa_ta

pud_ing

b_ll

an_el

CHRISTMAS CROSSWORD PUZZLE

Complete the puzzle below

XMAS CROSSWORD PUZZLE

Complete the puzzle below

1.

2.

3.

4.

5.

6.

CHRISTMAS CROSSWORD PUZZLE

Complete the puzzle below

Merry Christmas

HO HO HO

CHRISTMAS WORD SEARCH

Complete the word search puzzle below

MERRY CHRISTMAS!

Words go left, right, up, down, not diagonally, and can bend at a right angle.
There are no unused letters in the grid, every letter is used only once.

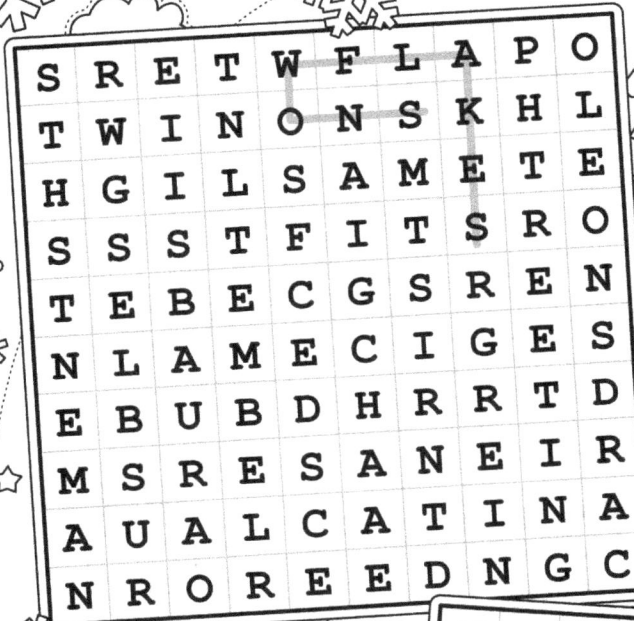

```
S  R  E  T  W  F  L  A  P  O
T  W  I  N  O  N  S  K  H  L
H  G  I  L  S  A  M  E  T  E
S  S  S  T  F  I  T  S  R  O
T  E  B  E  C  G  S  R  E  N
N  L  A  M  E  C  I  G  E  S
E  B  U  B  D  H  R  R  T  D
M  S  R  E  S  A  N  E  I  R
A  U  A  L  C  A  T  I  N  A
N  R  O  R  E  E  D  N  G  C
```

- BAUBLES
- CANDY CANE
- CAROLS
- CHRISTMAS LIGHTS
- CHRISTMAS TREE
- DECEMBER
- ELVES
- GIFTS
- GINGERBREAD
- GREETING CARDS
- HOLLY

- MISTLETOE
- NORTH POLE
- NUTCRACKER
- ORNAMENTS
- POINSETTIA
- REINDEER
- ROBIN
- SANTA CLAUS
- SNOWFLAKES
- SNOWMAN
- TOY FACTORY
- WINTER

```
E  R  O  W  M  A  N  R  B  R
K  S  N  T  S  I  M  E  G  E
C  A  R  L  E  T  O  E  N  A
H  C  C  T  U  N  S  S  I  D
R  S  E  T  T  I  E  L  G  E
I  N  I  O  P  A  V  O  C  N
S  T  M  A  S  E  L  R  A  A
T  E  E  R  T  Y  C  A  N  C
O  A  C  T  O  R  N  I  D  Y
Y  F  Y  L  L  O  H  B  O  R
```

ALL ABOUT SHAPES

Identify each shape. Trace, then color the shapes any color you like.

Square

Star

Circle

Pentagon

Triangle

Heptagon

Heart

Parallelogram

Oval

CHRISTMAS STOCKING

Color the shapes in the Christmas stocking. Follow the color scheme.

☆	○	☐	△
yellow	red	blue	green

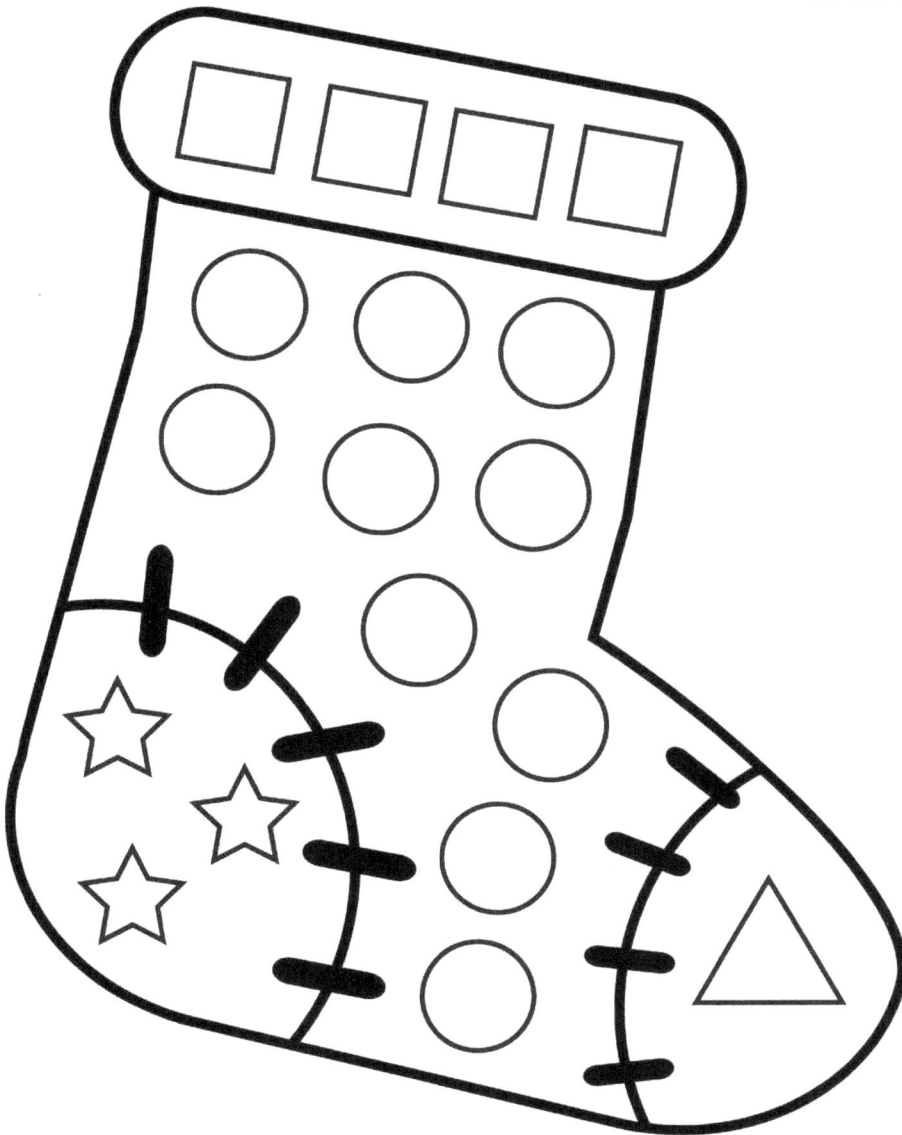

ODD ONE OUT

Circle the odd one out.

CHRISTMAS PATTERN

Draw what comes next in each row.

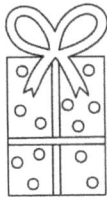

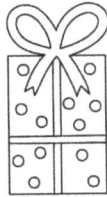

SCISSOR SKILLS

Carefully practice your scissor skills
cutting from the bottom to the stop sign.
Use age appropriate blunt end scissors

Parent: Cut out the sheet from the book first.

CHRISTMAS PRESENT

Cut along the dashed line.

Parent: Cut out the sheet from the book first.

SNOWMAN

Cut along the dashed line.

Parent: Cut out the sheet from the book first.

CANDY CANE

Cut along the dashed line.

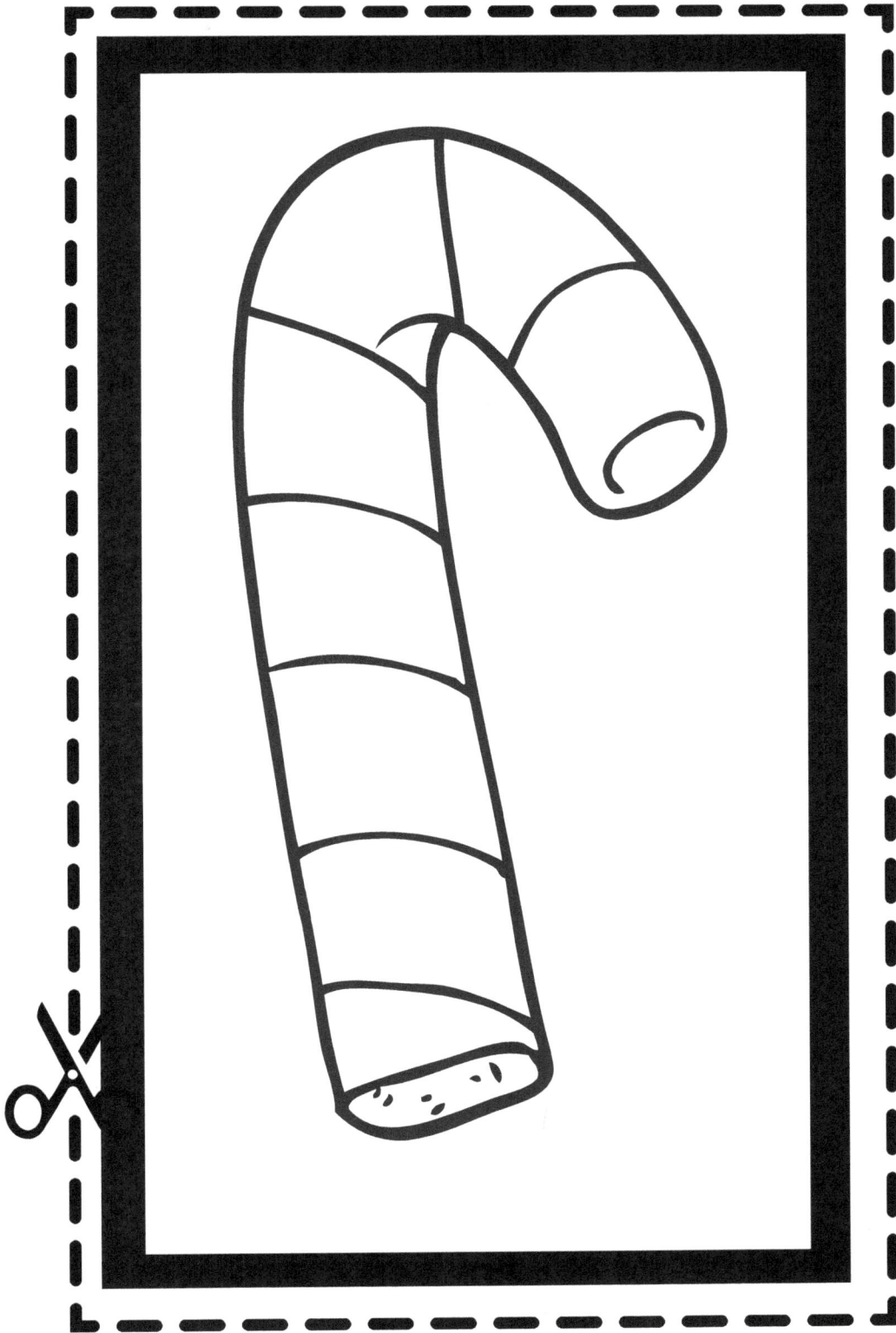

Parent: Cut out the sheet from the book first.

CHRISTMAS STOCKING

Cut along the dashed line.

Parent: Cut out the sheet from the book first.

CHRISTMAS WREATH

Cut along the dashed line.

Parent: Cut out the sheet from the book first.

CHRISTMAS PUDDING
Cut along the dashed line.

Parent: Cut out the sheet from the book first.

94

6-SIDED DICE

Cut out and glue to make a cube. Roll and say out loud the image it stops on.

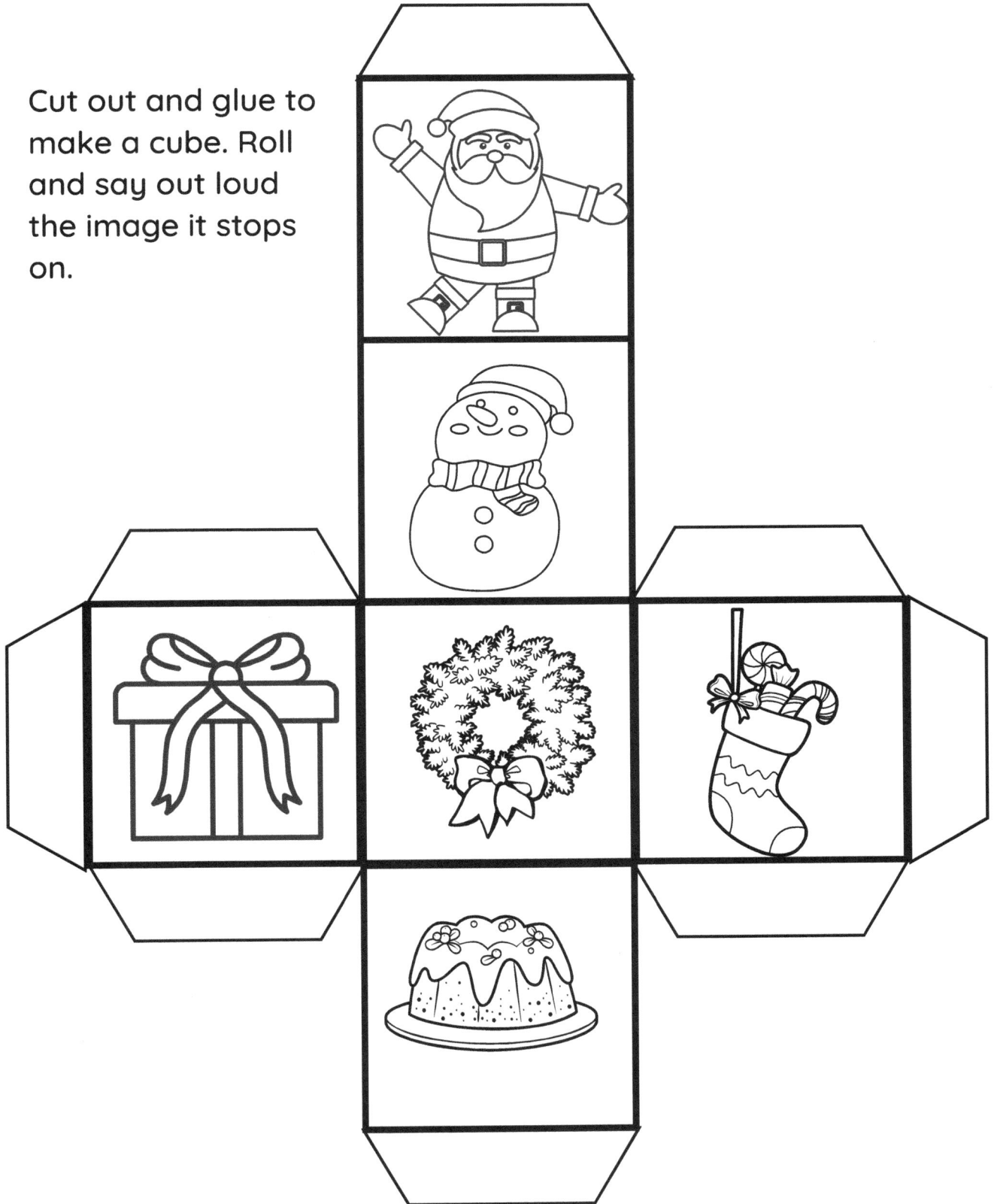

ANSWER KEYS

SANTA'S HERE YEA!
Guide Santa to the kids.

FROSTY THE SNOWMAN
Find the right shadow!

ANSWER: 1 - 3, 4 - 6, 5 - 2.

GUIDE SANTA!
Help Santa get to the house

WHO GETS THE GIFTS?
A, B or C?. Trace the line puzzles

PRESENT DELIVERY!
Guide Santa to the house.

SANTA'S SHADOW.
Find the right Santa

TREE ORNAMENTS.
Help the little girl get to the Christmas Tree

B IS FOR BELL
Circle the correct bell shadow

Bb

Trace and write the uppercase letter

Trace and write the lowercase letter

C IS FOR CANDY CANE
How many Candy canes do you see?

Cc

ANSWER: 12.

Trace and write the uppercase letter

Trace and write the lowercase letter

1

2

5

7

8

9

11

18

19

E IS FOR ELF
Help the elf load Santa's sleigh.

Ee

Trace and write the uppercase letter

Trace and write the lowercase letter

e e e e

21

H IS FOR HOLLY
Help the Elf get the holly

Hh

Trace and write the uppercase letter

Trace and write the lowercase letter

h h h

24

I IS FOR ICE SKATE
Trace a path through the maze. Use the ice skates

Ii

Answer:

Trace and write the uppercase letter

Trace and write the lowercase letter

25

K IS FOR KINGS
Guide the three wise men to the manger

Kk

Trace and write the uppercase letter

K K K K

Trace and write the lowercase letter

k k k k

27

L Is for Lights
Connect the dots A-L-I. Color the bulbs

Ll

Trace and write the uppercase letter

Trace and write the lowercase letter

28

M is for Mittens
Match the pairs of mittens. Spot the odd one out.

Mm

ANSWER:

Trace and write the uppercase letter

M M M M

Trace and write the lowercase letter

m m m m

29

O Is for Ornament
Find two identical ornaments

Oo

ANSWER:

Trace and write the uppercase letter

O O O O

Trace and write the lowercase letter

31

Q IS FOR QUINOA
Help Santa get to the Quinoa Salad!

Qq

Trace and write the uppercase letter

Q Q Q

Trace and write the lowercase letter

q q q q

33

R IS FOR RIBBON
Circle the correct ribbon shadow.

Rr

Trace and write the uppercase letter

R R R R

Trace and write the lowercase letter

r r r r

34

S IS FOR SANTA
Match each Santa to his shadow

Ss

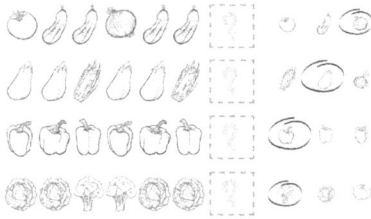

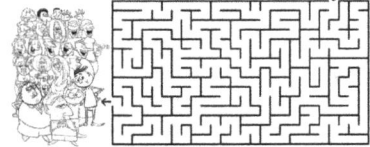

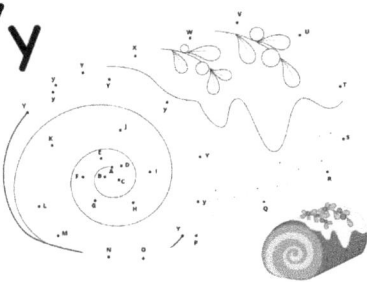

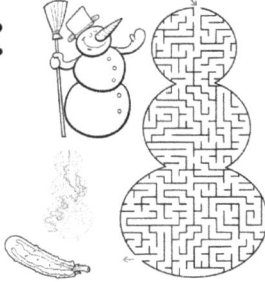

Trace and write the uppercase letter

Trace and write the lowercase letter

95

V IS FOR VEGETABLE
Circle the vegetable that comes next.

Vv

Trace and write the uppercase letter

Trace and write the lowercase letter

98

X Is for Xmas
Guide Santa to the Xmas party

Xx

Trace and write the uppercase letter

Trace and write the lowercase letter

40

Y IS FOR YULE LOG
Connect the dots A-Y-y for your Christmas dessert

Yy

Trace and write the uppercase letter

Trace and write the lowercase letter

41

Z IS FOR ZUCCHINI
Help the Snow man get his favorite vegetable

Zz

Trace and write the uppercase letter

Trace and write the lowercase letter

42

WHICH GIFT?
Color the gift with 1 written on it

1

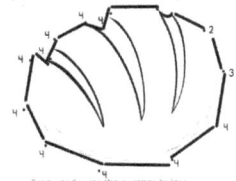

Trace and write the number below

one   **one**

Trace and write the word below

one one one one

47

HOW MANY ELVES?
Shade the circle with the right number of elves

2

1 2 3

Trace and write the number below

two   **two**

Trace and write the word below

two two two two

48

CHRISTMAS STOCKINGS
Find and circle 3 stockings

3

Trace and write the number below

three   **three**

Trace and write the word below

three three three

49

CHRISTMAS DINNER ROLL
1-4's dot to dot, to reveal a sweet dinner roll.

4

Trace and write the number below

four   **four**

Trace and write the word below

four four four

50

Snow Fight!
There are 5 differences. Circle each one.

5

Trace and write the number below

five   **five**

Trace and write the word below

51

LOST NOSE
Help the snowman get to the carrot

6

Trace and write the number below

six   **six**

Trace and write the word below

52

SANTA CONVENTION!
Find and circle 7 differences!

7

Trace and write the number below

seven   **seven**

Trace and write the word below

53

TEN?
YES! Find 10 differences between the two pictures.

10

Trace and write the number below

ten   **ten**

Trace and write the word below

56

CHRISTMAS BOWS.
Count and record

ANSWER: 8.

57

CHRISTMAS ELEMENTS
Count each row of images. Write the correct number in the circle.

5

4

3

5

4

6

58

CANDLES, MITTENS, AND MORE!
Count the Christmas object in each box and mark the correct number

4 (1) 3 2   2 (3) 5 7

2 1 (5) 4   8 7 (4) 3

59

TWO SETS OF SANTA?
Count the 2 Santa images. Record your number.

21
19

61

CHRISTMAS PRESENT.
Find 10 differences.

1
2
3
4
5
6
7
8
9
10

63

CHRISTMAS MITTEN.
Compare the two images

2 3 1
5 4
7
6 8 9
9
10

BEGINNING LETTER
Identify each image out loud. Say the letter it begins with.
Color the letter it begins with.

b o c s
p b n t
r e s a
h s p o
w b m p

MATCH & TRACE
Name the image. Match the image with the first letter of the word.
Trace the uppercase and lowercase letters.

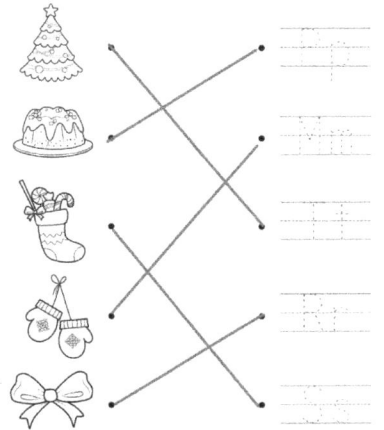

PRACTICE TRACING.
Trace and connect words to Christmas elements.

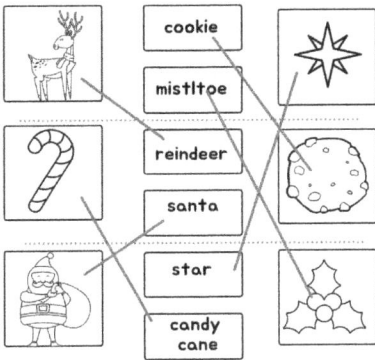

cookie
mistltoe
reindeer
santa
star
candy cane

RHYMING WORDS
Circle the word that rhymes with the word inside the box.

sled	hug	bread
tree	flea	yam
sock	see	clock
candle	handle	bend
bell	shell	skid
wreath	pen	teeth

CHRISTMAS WORD SALAD
Identify the image. Unscramble the letters.

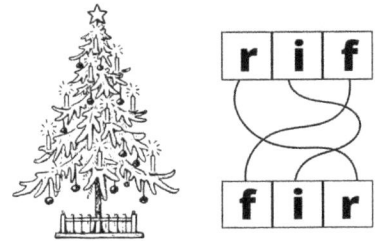

r i f
f i r

XMAS WORD SALAD
Identify the scene. Unscramble the words.

t v y i a i n t
n a t i v i t y

MISSING LETTERS
Identify each image below. Write the missing letter.

sweater   gift   frosty
sleigh   snow   santa
pudding   bell   angel

CHRISTMAS CROSSWORD PUZZLE
Complete the puzzle below

1. Mitten 2. Present 3. Bell 4. Star
5. (across) Snowflake 5. (down) Santa
6. Fireplace 7. Cookie 8. Snowman
9. Tree 10. Hat 11. Ball 12. Candle

66   67   68

69   70   71

72   79   74

XMAS CROSSWORD PUZZLE
Complete the puzzle below

1.
2.
3.
4.
5.
6.

ANSWER: 1.Snowglobe 2.Deer 3.Present 4.Snowman 5.Stocking 6.Santa

75

CHRISTMAS CROSSWORD PUZZLE
Complete the puzzle below

Merry Christmas
HO HO HO

1.Santa 2.Snowman 3.Bear 4.Tree
5.Owl 6.Reindeer 7.Penguin
8.Bird 9.Mittens 10.Cookie

76

CHRISTMAS WORD SEARCH
Complete the puzzle below

MERRY CHRISTMAS!
Words go left, right, up, down, not diagonally, and can bend at a right angle.
There are no unused letters in the grid, every letter is used only once.

S R E T W F L A P O
T W I N O N S K H L
H G I L S A M E T E
S S S T F I T S R O
T E B E C G S R E N
N L A M E C I G E S
E B U B D H R R T D
M S R E S A N E I R
A U A L C A T I N A
N R O R E E D N G C

E R O W M A N R B R
K S N T S I M E G E
C A R L E T O E N A
H C C T U N S S I D
R S E T T I E L G E
I N I O P A V O C N
S T M A S E L R A C
T E E R T Y C A N C
Q A C T O R N I D Y
Y F Y L L O H B O R

BAUBLES
CANDY CANE
CAROLS
CHRISTMAS LIGHTS
CHRISTMAS TREE
DECEMBER
ELVES
GIFTS
GINGERBREAD
GREETING CARDS
HOLLY

MISTLETOE
NORTH POLE
NUTCRACKER
ORNAMENTS
POINSETTIA
REINDEER
ROBIN
SANTA CLAUS
SNOWFLAKES
SNOWMAN
TOY FACTORY
WINTER

ANSWER:

77

ODD ONE OUT
Circle the odd one out.

80

CHRISTMAS PATTERN
Draw what comes next in each row.

81

More books by Mare

☑ Scan the QR Code with your phones camera

☑ Click on the link

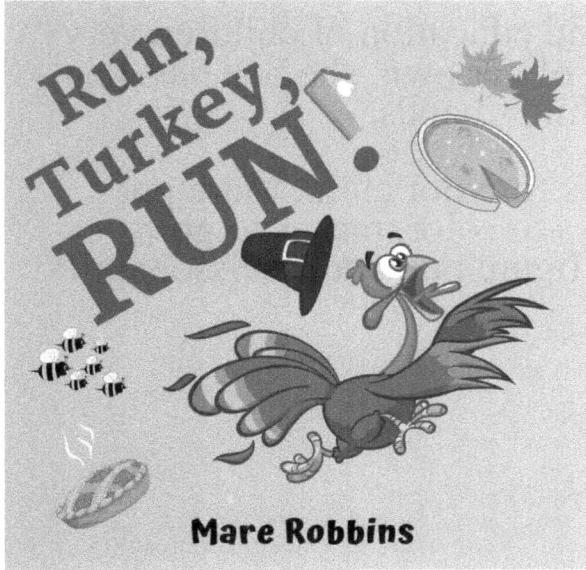

Run, Turkey, RUN!
Mare Robbins

Amazon

Barnes and Noble

Thanksgiving PRESCHOOL Activity Book
LETTERS ABC
WORDS Pumpkin
90 + Thanksgiving Themed Games!
Start
Mare Robbins

Amazon

Barnes and Noble

ABOUT THE AUTHOR

Mare Robbins has the development and education of children very close to her heart. With three children of her own, she believes that it's never too early to put a book in a child's hands.

To help you provide engaging activities for your child, Mare put together this practical book with images to color, mazes to go through, shapes to identify, puzzles to figure out, and a scissor skill practice section!

www.ingramcontent.com/pod-product-compliance
Lightning Source LLC
Chambersburg PA
CBHW062001090426
42811CB00006B/1004